Allergy-Free *and* Easy Cooking

Allergy-Free
and Easy Cooking

30-minute meals without gluten, wheat, dairy, eggs,
soy, peanuts, tree nuts, fish, shellfish, and sesame

CYBELE PASCAL

photography by Chugrad McAndrews

TEN SPEED PRESS
Berkeley

The information contained in this book is based on the experience and research of the author. It is not intended as a substitute for consulting with your physician or other health-care provider. Any attempt to diagnose and treat an illness should be done under the direction of a health-care professional. The publisher and author are not responsible for any adverse effects or consequences resulting from the use of any of the suggestions, preparations, or procedures discussed in this book.

Published in the United States by Ten Speed Press, an imprint of the Crown Publishing Group, a division of Random House, Inc., New York.

www.crownpublishing.com

www.tenspeed.com

Ten Speed Press and the Ten Speed Press colophon are registered trademarks of Random House, Inc.

Library of Congress Cataloging-in-Publication Data is on file with the publisher

ISBN 978-1-60774-291-3
eISBN 978-1-60774-292-0

Printed in China

Design by Sarah Pulver

10 9 8 7 6 5 4 3 2 1

First Edition

This book is dedicated to my late mother-in-law, Wendy,
who bought me my first Vidalia Chop Wizard,
and to my mother, Susanna, and my father, Eric,
who started me peeling carrots when I was three years old.

Contents

Foreword

It was a cold and Chicago-crisp Christmas morning. The sky was piercing blue and the snow was blown in gentle drifts. My family was all gathered together at the table and before we ate the beautiful breakfast that sat in front of us, I raised my glass to toast someone. In a Midwest condo, on Christmas morning, a family with three severely food-allergic children was toasting Cybele, a woman we had never even met who lives across the country. We were toasting her because we were eating milk-free, wheat-free, soy-free, nut-free, egg-free vanilla scones and we were eating those scones together. Let me explain.

We have a family tradition that we all sleep at the same house on Christmas Eve so that we can wake up together on Christmas morning and share the joy of giving and receiving. For the first four years after the children were diagnosed with multiple food allergies, we did just that . . . except that as soon as the gifts were opened, the rest of my family promptly left. They didn't leave because they wanted to, they left because they had to. The food that I was about to whip up for breakfast would be nearly inedible.

You see, I didn't expect to be cooking top eight allergen-free. I didn't expect to be making every single breakfast, lunch, and dinner at home. In fact, I didn't expect to be at home for lunch at all. After my pediatric residency training at Children's Memorial Hospital (CMH), Chicago, I completed an allergy/immunology fellowship at CMH and Northwestern Memorial Hospital, Chicago. Around this time, I found that three of my four children had such severe food allergies that I felt that I had no choice but to stay home with them. I couldn't see myself at work taking care of children with allergic disease while my own children were carrying the burden of allergic disease themselves, requiring daily antihistamines, steroid creams, and, all too often, epinephrine. I didn't feel like I could create a safe enough environment in which to leave them. So I put my career as a food allergy expert in the hospital on hold and instead became a food allergy expert in my own home and in my own kitchen.

Oh, my kitchen. My newly, and quite forcefully, arranged marriage to the kitchen has easily been the most challenging lifestyle change to which I have had to adjust. Having children with multiple food allergies literally plopped me in the center of a world that was completely unfamiliar to me. I was entirely lost in the company of pots and pans, peelers and processors.

Don't get me wrong; I enjoy food. I enjoy good food. In fact, I have historically been a pretty big eater. But when we were growing up, my sisters were the ones to help my mom cook and bake. That simply wasn't my job. I did not envy their cute aprons. I did not want to crack eggs. I didn't want to poke the cake with a toothpick (I didn't know what in the world that was supposed to tell you anyway). I had no desire to join them. I would help my dad clear the table, and I was very good at running to the grocery store to pick up missing and necessary ingredients. I loved and was good at these jobs. All this is to say that food preparation does not come easily to me. I wouldn't do it unless I was forced. And then, there I was. Being forced.

Being a pediatric allergist provided me with no training in how to cook for my own food-allergic children. My mom was my savior and constant companion in the kitchen since the minute I was forced there, but both she and I were running out of ideas. We were on our own until my friend bought me Cybele Pascal's *Allergen-Free Baker's Handbook*. I figured my friend had wasted her money, as I had done so many times, on cookbooks that were way too complicated for the novice and filled with recipes that could not ever have been taste-tested. Boy, Cybele proved me wrong! Every recipe in that cookbook is both delectable and well loved by my family. We often can be found eating Blueberry Boy Bait several days a week!

But my children are ever hungry and we've become busier and busier. They've got soccer and basketball, all at different times. I've got school pick-up during that crucial hour before I put dinner on the table. I needed more quick, go-to meals that were equal parts efficient and delicious. When Cybele told me this was exactly what she was creating, I realized she knows me without ever having met me in person. She knows what food-allergic families want and need. We can't get enough of her Chicken Tenders, and I made the Shepherd's Pie thinking I would have leftovers, but every last bite was nibbled up! I can make each of these amazing meals in about thirty minutes, and that's with four little kids climbing the cabinets, asking to help stir, and begging me to hurry because they're starving! She's even got me wearing an apron. I couldn't ask for anything more.

Thank you, Cybele. That early morning holiday toast to you was only the first of many.

Sarah M. Boudreau-Romano, MD, FAAP
The Allergist Mom, LLC
TheAllergistMom.com

Introduction:
Free *and* Easy *for* All

This book is for all of you out there who might not feel like cooking tonight. I know: I've been there, time and time again. For many people, when you don't feel like making dinner, you just order takeout. Or you go out. Or you defrost something from the freezer. But what about those of us living with food allergies or food intolerances? Just picking up the phone and ordering Chinese food is not an option. So, most often, we have to cook, even when we really don't feel like it. This book, comrades, is for you. It's a collection of seventy-five allergy-free but flavor-full meals that can be whipped up in thirty minutes or less, to help simplify your complicated life. As a working mother, I know that most nights the last thing I want to do is spend an hour or more preparing dinner. I just don't have the time, energy, or inspiration. But like it or not, I've got a food-allergic household, and something safe, healthy, and delicious has got to land on that table.

I've often thought, "Wouldn't it be great if someone came up with a guidebook for day-to-day allergy-free cooking?" I've also spent many years asking my readers what recipes they miss most. This book is that guidebook,

and a collection of those recipes, all designed to answer the most frequent request of all: "Make it fast, make it simple!" These seventy-five completely allergy-free meals will take the guesswork out of meal planning for you. These are the foods you love. Comfort foods. Not weird food, just good food that is also allergy-free; every recipe is free of gluten, dairy, eggs, soy, peanuts, tree nuts, fish, shellfish, and sesame, so you don't have to make substitutions. And all without the slightest sacrifice of taste or texture. In fact, I've been told by those with no food restrictions that these recipes are better than the "originals." So, whatever your allergies or intolerances, there's something in here for you. And all cooked up in thirty minutes or less.

In this book, I share my favorite secrets for turning allergenic recipes into allergy-free cuisine. There is an alchemy to allergy-free cooking; I've spent ten years refining my understanding of it, and here, I teach you the magic behind the mystery. I'll teach you how to take rice milk and brown rice flour and transform it into a cream sauce. How to take olive oil and rice milk and transform it into an egg. I know most of you can make a salad allergy-free, but wouldn't you love to be able to make creamy mac 'n' cheese without wheat, gluten, dairy, or soy? My last book, the *Allergen-Free Baker's Handbook*, taught people how to bake without wheat, eggs, and dairy, the three mainstays of traditional baking. This book will teach you how to make grilled cheese without cheese, pizza without wheat, and pesto without nuts, just to name a few. With these recipes, you'll be eating all your family favorites again in no time.

This collection of beloved recipe classics is for the fifteen million Americans living with food allergies. In the United States, one out of every thirteen kids under the age of eighteen has a food allergy. This book is also for the estimated 30 percent of Americans living with gluten intolerance, and the one in a hundred living with celiac disease. We have a lot of mouths to feed safely.

I wrote this book for you, and for me. Because like you, my circumstances dictate that I must cook something safe and healthy, whether I feel like it or not.

My son Lennon was diagnosed with severe multiple food allergies at four months old. He outgrew his dairy and soy allergies by the time he was six. However, he was then diagnosed with shellfish, tree nut, and kiwi allergies, which I'm assuming are for life. My other son, Monte, has allergic asthma and must avoid dairy when it flares; he was also diagnosed with a shellfish allergy last year. I myself have fish, shellfish, tree nut, wheat, and a variety of fruit allergies. My husband is dairy-allergic and gluten-intolerant. And so, we continue to eat allergy-free.

Now, I'm a foodie, but as my kids have grown older, and the homework load has gotten intense, and I am working around the clock, and my husband is often somewhere else, working just as hard, I don't have time to cook the way I used to. I will not be making slow-braised short ribs, or lamb that has to marinate for two days. Like you, I want quick and easy recipes that taste good. And of course I need them to be healthy and allergy-free, too. So I wrote the book I needed but couldn't find.

Allergy-Free and Easy Cooking is for those learning to cook and those who love to cook. It's also for you if you hate to cook but have to: hopefully, it will help you like it a little better.

Stocking Your Kitchen *for* Quick *and* Easy Allergy-Free Cooking

A well-stocked pantry means fewer trips to the grocery store and makes it much easier to whip up dinner on the spur of the moment. The following shelf-stable pantry items and equipment will keep your shopping to the minimum while maximizing your options.

INGREDIENTS

If you've used either of my previous cookbooks, some of these ingredients may look familiar, like my favorite superfine brown rice flour from Authentic Foods. Others will be new, like coconut amino acids and brown rice bowls. Most of these items are available at Whole Foods, your local natural foods market, or online. See the Resources for more information about allergy-friendly products and brands that I have found and that I use.

Agave nectar
A lightly floral, nutritive, unrefined sweetener that is low on the glycemic index. A little added to soups or sauces counteracts bitterness.

Artichoke hearts (in water and/or marinated)
Great for quick pasta or chicken dishes.

Baking spray
Canola oil or olive oil baking spray is great for oiling pans. Many brands contain soy lecithin, however. If this is a problem for you, substitute plain canola oil or olive oil.

Balsamic vinegar
A great flavor booster when you are short on time, because you don't have to simmer it in sauces for long periods, like you do with wine. Also, an essential salad dressing ingredient. A little bit goes a long way.

Broth
Chicken (regular and low-sodium), vegetable, and beef broth are always good to keep on hand. Kitchen Basics broths are allergy-free (see Resources).

Brown rice bowls
Precooked, shelf-stable brown rice bowls simplify life by shaving off forty-five minutes of cooking time.

Brown rice flour (superfine)
One of the most important ingredients in your allergy-friendly pantry is Authentic Foods brand superfine brown rice flour. It has a lovely mild flavor, and none of the grittiness one usually associates with rice flour. It is my favorite brand. Ener-G brown rice flour and King Arthur brown rice flour are also good, and both are manufactured in dedicated allergy-free facilities. It's the secret behind allergy-friendly "cream" sauce, fluffy biscuits, and creamy soup, gravy, and stew. See Resources.

Buckwheat groats (kasha)
Buckwheat groats are a great whole grain gluten-free alternative to couscous, bulgur wheat, and so on. They are often used in Eastern European cooking, but also do very well in Mediterranean dishes.

Canned beans
Canned beans are a fantastic time-saver when you are whipping up vegan meals. I always keep a good supply of kidney beans, chickpeas, black beans, cannellini (white) beans, black-eyed peas, and pinto beans. They are endlessly useful. See Resources for BPA-free brands.

Canned corn
If you can eat corn, it's great to keep canned sweet corn on hand for adding to things like chili. My kids also like it warmed up as a simple side. Look for GMO-free corn, and see Resources for BPA-free brands.

Canned flaked chicken and turkey
Canned chicken and turkey are great for spur of the moment food preparation, and are also handy for any recipe where you'd traditionally use canned flaked tuna, such as Chicken Noodle Casserole (page 66). See Resources for BPA-free brands.

Canned roasted green chiles
A Southwestern staple that's great in bean or meat dishes. Roasted chiles add depth of flavor without a lot of additional salt. They come in mild, medium, or hot.

Canned tomatoes
Tomatoes are a rich source of vitamin C and lycopene, both powerful antioxidants. I use tomatoes in myriad ways, and I keep a plentiful supply of whole plum tomatoes, crushed tomatoes, tomato sauce, tomato paste, pureed tomatoes, diced tomatoes, diced roasted tomatoes, and diced roasted tomatoes with chiles. You will use them all. See Resources for recommended BPA-free brands.

Canola oil
A mild, neutral-flavored oil that is great for cooking. In my quest to find a vegetable oil that is free of any risk of cross-contamination with allergenic oils such as peanut, tree nut, soy, or sesame oil, the only one I have been able to find

(other than olive oil) with a safety assurance is Crisco canola oil). You may also use sunflower or safflower oil in place of canola oil.

Choice Batter
This product is an amazing innovation in gluten-free cooking that is used for battering and frying; it absorbs 50 percent less oil than normal batter. See Resources for sourcing information.

Cider vinegar
A gluten-free vinegar made from apple cider. It is milder than red wine vinegar or balsamic vinegar, and also great in place of lemon if you can't eat citrus.

Coconut
Unsweetened coconut chips and unsweetened shredded coconut are nice additions to curries and rice dishes (see Resources).

Coconut amino acids
This brilliant addition to the gluten-free, soy-free pantry will change your life when it comes to making Asian food. While not exactly like soy sauce, it's a pretty good stand-in, and if you use it in one of my sauces, you'll be swearing it's the real thing. See Resources.

Coconut milk
Coconut milk is a sweet, creamy vegan "milk" derived from the meat of a mature coconut. It is excellent in place of dairy cream, and it adds richness to sauces. It comes in cans, which you need to shake vigorously before opening to mix the rich cream in with the liquid (the cream rises to the top inside the can). See Resources for recommended BPA-free brands.

A Note on Coconut

I do not consider coconut a tree nut, and neither does the Food Allergy & Anaphylaxis Network/Food Allergy Initiative (FAAN/FAI) or the American Academy of Allergy, Asthma & Immunology (AAAAI). Dr. Hugh Sampson, professor of pediatrics and chief of the division of allergy and immunology in the department of pediatrics at the Mount Sinai School of Medicine in New York City, where he also serves as director of the Jaffe Food Allergy Institute, says, "Coconut is not a nut but the seed of a drupaceous fruit. We have not restricted our nut allergic patients of coconut, and have not seen a problem. If there is any question about coconut reactivity, we test for it and occasionally have found a coconut allergic patient."

However, in 2006 the FDA began mandating that coconut be considered a tree nut for labeling purposes. No one is sure how they came to this conclusion, and several food industry sources are asking them to revise this classification. As FAAN notes, coconut allergies are exceedingly rare. The available medical literature documents only a small number of allergic reactions to coconut, and most occurred in people who were not allergic to other tree nuts. Therefore, I have used coconut in a few of the recipes in this book. I don't think it's fair to deprive people of such a healthful and delicious ingredient because the FDA has erroneously classified a fruit as a nut. But please err on the side of caution, and ask your doctor if you need to avoid coconut before making a coconut recipe.

Cornflakes
Cornflakes are great for breading, or as a filler and binder, in the place of breadcrumbs. See Resources for recommended brands.

Cornmeal

Dried corn ground to fine, medium, or coarse texture. Cornmeal is available in yellow, white, and blue. It's great for gluten-free baking, and it's a key ingredient in my deep dish pizza crust.

Cornstarch (organic, GMO-free)

A versatile starch that is great in sauces as a thickening and binding agent. Potato starch and tapioca starch can generally be substituted one for one if you can't eat corn products. See Resources for recommended brands.

Dried fruits

Apricots, cherries, cranberries, currants, dates, figs, raisins, and so on. They're each great mixed into grain dishes, and they're wonderful as an unrefined sweetener pureed in sauces.

Egg replacer

I recommend Ener-G brand egg replacer. Please note that "egg substitute" is not the same thing as "egg replacer." Egg substitute often contains egg whites, and is therefore not suitable for those with egg allergies or vegans.

Garfava or chickpea flour

High-fiber, high-protein, gluten-free bean flour.

Gluten-free breadcrumbs

There are two types of gluten-free breadcrumbs on the market—corn-based and rice-based. Both have their place. The corn-based ones are generally better for breading, while the very fine rice breadcrumbs are great for adding to things like pesto as a thickener. I use gluten-free breadcrumbs in many ways, from breading chicken to adding crunch to toppings to beefing up Salisbury steak.

Gluten-free pasta

About as essential as sleep. My kids eat pasta almost every day. There are so many great options out there for gluten-free pasta these days, in almost every shape. Stock up, it's cheap! See Resources for recommended brands.

Herbs and spices

Dried herbs and spices are a mainstay for quick and easy cooking. They add flavor, and having a well-stocked supply saves you from emergency shopping trips. Some essentials are dried oregano, dried thyme, dried rosemary, ground cumin, paprika (sweet, hot, and smoked), chili powder, ground chile pepper (cayenne, ancho, chipotle, and so on), black pepper (whole peppercorns and ground pepper), ground white pepper, ground cinnamon, ground nutmeg, ground allspice, barbecue seasoning, poultry seasoning, garlic powder, onion powder, and bay leaves.

Honey

A little bit of honey in soup or a sauce adds an extra layer of flavor that can't be identified, but is that special bit of oomph. Honey, if local, is also said to help fight seasonal allergies.

Instant polenta

Instant Italian dinner! My family loves polenta; it cooks in literally minutes, and is a great alternative to mashed potatoes. Serve it with a little Earth Balance soy-free buttery spread, or any of the red sauces in this book.

Jams and jellies

A little jam or jelly can be the secret behind a fabulous pork or chicken dish. I like to keep apricot and cherry jam on my shelves for suppertime dishes. (And strawberry and raspberry for the morning.)

Ketchup
Organic gluten-free ketchup is one of my favorite secret ingredients. I often prefer it to tomato paste in sauces, because it's not as bitter. A little dash'll do you. And of course, it's necessary to have on hand for those ubiquitous hot dogs and hamburgers and, if you're like my kids, chicken tenders, too.

Millet
Millet is an ancient grain that is finally coming back into fashion. It's high protein and quick cooking and has a mild nutty flavor that is lovely anywhere you'd use couscous or rice. (Pictured at right.)

Molasses
A rich, nutritive, unrefined sweetener.

Olive oil
You will want to keep both a mild olive oil and a more flavorful extra virgin olive oil in your cupboards. Regular olive oil is great for cooking because of its neutral taste, while extra virgin is good for dressings and sauces when you want to taste some olive oil flavor.

Potato starch
A great thickening agent. It is not the same as potato flour, which is a much denser flour with a distinct potato flavor. Potato starch is light, fluffy, and very mild in flavor. The difference between the two is akin to cornstarch and cornmeal.

Quinoa
A high protein, fiber-rich heirloom grain that is extremely quick cooking.

Red wine vinegar
Like balsamic vinegar, red wine vinegar added to sauce or chili will stand in for red wine, and it cooks much more quickly. It's also a great addition to dressings for Mediterranean salads.

Rice
All varieties: brown, basmati, jasmine, long grain white, and so on.

Rice milk
A light, delicate, plant-based milk that is great for sauces and soups. Look for gluten-free, enriched brands (see Resources).

Rice noodles

These come in various forms—maifun (angel hair), pad Thai, and so on.

Rice vinegar

Milder than balsamic or red wine vinegar, or even distilled white vinegar. It is an essential in my kitchen. I opt for the unseasoned kind, instead of the one that's loaded with sodium.

Salt

Fine sea salt, coarse sea salt, kosher salt, and table salt are good types to have on hand. I use fine sea salt because it is more nutritive than table salt, but they are interchangeable, so feel free to use table salt, unless otherwise specified in a recipe.

Seaweed

Use kombu (kelp) to make soy-free soy sauce and flavorful broths; it's a great source of umami— the rich, full taste that comes from amino acids in foods. (My kids also love seaweed snacks for their lunchboxes.)

Sugar

Brown sugar and natural cane sugar are great flavor boosters in sauces; you only need a little.

Sunflower seeds

Sunflower seeds are considered to be one of the world's healthiest foods. They are very rich in vitamin E and vitamin B (thiamin). In recent years, they have been touted as a great substitute for peanuts and tree nuts for those with food allergies.

Sunflower seed butter (SunButter)

SunButter comes in crunchy and smooth styles and can be used in all the ways you'd traditionally use nut butters. It is also nutritionally superior to peanut butter.

Taco shells

My kids go back and forth between requesting hard tacos and soft tacos. Best to keep both taco shells and tortillas on hand, so you can make either type of taco at the drop of a hat.

Tapioca flour (tapioca starch)

A mild, starchy flour made from the cassava root that is extremely versatile. It's great for thickening sauces, coating chicken tenders, and it's a key ingredient in my Basic Gluten-Free Flour Mix.

Tortilla chips

Great for dipping or scooping chili, as well as in nachos or Tex-Mex Casserole (page 65).

Vegetable shortening, dairy-free, soy-free

I recommend Spectrum Naturals organic vegetable shortening, made from palm oil. It is the most consistent and stable of the dairy-free, soy-free vegetable shortenings on the market (in my opinion).

Xanthan gum

A plant product that mimics gluten. It provides structure and elasticity in baking, but also acts as a great emulsifier in sauces and dressings. A little bit goes a long way, so measure it carefully

THE PERISHABLE GOODS PANTRY

For the recipes in this book, you will want to shop the produce section wisely to maximize time-saving. Look for shortcut items, like shredded cabbage, carrot and celery sticks, chopped onions, sliced mushrooms, sliced bell peppers, and diced butternut squash. These prepped veggies can cut your total kitchen time in half, if not more.

While individual recipes will call for you to buy specific ingredients, the following perishable items are good to keep stocked in your fridge (or freezer or pantry, where noted), because you will be using them regularly.

Allergy-friendly bread and buns
Store back-up breads in the freezer.

Bacon
Choose nitrite-free.

Capers
Choose nonpareils (the smaller ones).

Carrots

Celery

Chicken
I call for breasts, tenders, cutlets, thighs, and split breasts in this book; store in the freezer if not using immediately.

Cooked chicken
Rotisserie, grilled, steamed, and so on—can be a real time-saver.

Corn tortillas

Daiya vegan cheese, shredded: cheddar, mozzarella, and pepperjack
Store unopened in the refrigerator; once opened, store in the freezer if not using within a week, particularly pepperjack, which spoils easily. Sliced Daiya vegan cheeses and wedges of Daiya are available at the deli counter at Whole Foods.

Dijon mustard

Earth Balance soy-free buttery spread

Flaxseed and flaxseed meal
Both flaxseed and flaxseed meal are rich in omega-3s. Flaxseed meal mixed with hot water can stand in for eggs in vegan baking. Store it in the fridge or freezer, or it will go rancid quickly.

Fresh chile peppers
Jalapeños, serranos, habaneros, Thai chiles, and so on.

Fresh herbs
Rosemary, thyme, basil, parsley, cilantro, mint, and so on.

Frozen vegetables
Spinach, corn, mixed peas and carrots, sweet peas, pearl onions, and so on.

Fruits
Assorted fresh and frozen; some, like bananas, do need to be stored outside the fridge.

Garlic
Do not store in the refrigerator, but rather in a cool dark place like the pantry.

Gingerroot

Gluten-free tortillas
There are great brown rice tortillas and other gluten-free options.

Green onions

Ground beef
Store in the freezer if not using immediately.

Ground bison or buffalo
Store in the freezer if not using immediately.

Ground dark meat turkey
Store in the freezer if not using immediately.

Hemp seeds, shelled (hemp hearts)
Store in the freezer or fridge once open.

Hot sauce
Tabasco, Louisiana, Sriracha, for example; store in the fridge once open.

Italian sausage, hot and sweet
Store in the freezer if not using immediately.

Lemongrass

Lemons

Limes

Mirin
Japanese cooking wine made from rice; store in the fridge once open.

Mushroom broth
A rich, flavorful vegan broth that stands in for soy sauce in Asian dishes.

Olives
Kalamata, green, and black; whole, pitted, and sliced.

Onions
Yellow, sweet, and red. Do not store in the refrigerator, but rather in a cool dark place like the pantry.

Pickapeppa Sauce
A great allergy-friendly stand-in for Worcestershire sauce.

Pork chops, pork tenderloin
Store in the freezer if not using immediately.

Potatoes
Do not store these in the refrigerator, but rather in a cool dark place like the pantry.

Precut vegetables
See the list of frozen vegetables on page 19.

Rice milk
Refrigerate after opening.

Roasted red peppers
Jarred Mediterranean or Turkish or roasted red bell peppers.

Sweet potatoes
Do not store these in the refrigerator but rather in a cool dark place like the pantry.

Vegan soy-free mayonnaise
Store in the fridge once open.

Yogurt, vegan, plain: coconut milk or rice milk
I like So Delicious plain coconut milk yogurt best.

Substituting the Substitutions

If you want to add back in any of the allergenic ingredients, please read the following.

- For any recipe calling for vegan nondairy milk, you may use cow's milk or soy milk instead, one for one.

- For any recipe using superfine brown rice flour, you may use all-purpose flour instead, one for one.

- For any recipe calling for an olive oil/ rice milk emulsion for coating cutlets or tenders, you may use a beaten egg instead. One tablespoon of rice milk mixed with 2 tablespoons of olive oil is equivalent to 1 egg. For any 1½ teaspoons of Ener-G egg replacer mixed with 2 tablespoons of rice milk, you may substitute 1 egg.

- For any recipe using shortening or Earth Balance soy-free buttery spread, you may use butter or soy-based margarine, one for one, instead.

- For any recipe calling for gluten-free pasta, you may use regular semolina pasta instead, one for one, but please note that cooking times may vary, so check the packaging.

- For peanuts, tree nuts, sesame, fish, and shellfish, use at your own discretion, and check with your physician or allergist.

ALCOHOL

I sometimes use a little gluten-free alcohol in my cooking. It adds a boost of flavor, and the alcohol itself cooks out. All distilled alcohols are gluten-free, as are all types of wine, including those listed below. Luckily, gluten-free beer is also very easy to find these days. Look for Bard's Tale or Redbridge, which are both widely available.

Dry sherry

Gluten-free beer

Port

Red wine

Sweet Marsala

White wine

EQUIPMENT

Here's the deal you and I are going make: if you want to clock in at thirty minutes or less on these recipes, you will need to stock your kitchen with a few time-saver tools. These are modern convenience items that will simplify your life tremendously. If you don't heed my recommendations here, I can't guarantee you'll be rolling out supper in half an hour. These recipes were developed with these tools, and when I give recipe preparation and cooking times, I'm assuming you'll be using them too. Without the tools, the recipes are still simple, but you'll have longer prep time, and sometimes longer cooking time.

THE TOP SIX MOST IMPORTANT KITCHEN GADGETS AND SMALL APPLIANCES

Food processor with multiple blades
A kitchen essential that is great for grating carrots, onions, and apples, shredding cabbage, chopping veggies, pulsing to make breadcrumbs, pureeing, and so on. Its uses are endless.

Garlic press
Use this tool to prepare garlic in one second, instead of mincing it with a knife.

Immersion blender
The handheld stick blender, or immersion blender, is a favorite of mine. It saves you from washing extra equipment, and it saves time. Just stick the blender in your pot and puree or liquefy the contents. No need to transfer to a jar blender and then transfer back again.

Microwave oven
I know most people have microwaves these days, but just in case you don't, I thought I'd include this. These recipes have been developed with the assumption that you have one. They make it possible to whip up shepherd's pie, paella, and risotto in thirty minutes or less.

Mini chopper
Another super handy way to mince garlic, fresh ginger, fresh chiles, and so on in a matter of seconds.

Vidalia Chop Wizard
This is my very favorite gadget. It dices veggies, from onions to peppers to celery to carrots, in a matter of seconds. A truly brilliant invention, and beyond worth the twenty dollar investment. Get it at Target, Bed Bath & Beyond, or on Amazon (see Resources).

Important Tips for Successful Cooking

1. Please read the recipe all the way through at least once before making it.

2. Measure out all your ingredients before you start.

3. Invest in a good digital timer, so cooking times are exact.

4. Use good quality pans that are the appropriate kind, size, and weight for the recipe.

5. Use nesting measuring cups for solids and glass measuring cups for liquids.

6. For accuracy, check the level of liquid ingredients at eye level from the side.

MEASURING TOOLS

Dry measuring cups
For measuring solid and semisolid ingredients; these allow you to level ingredients with a straightedge.

Liquid measuring cups
These allow you to read measurements from the side, and have a spout for pouring.

Measuring spoons
Invest in a good set; you'll use them forever.

Retractable cookie scoop
A 2-tablespoon retractable cookie scoop simplifies making meatballs.

KNIVES

Chopping knife (8-inch or 9-inch chef's knife)
For chopping and cutting.

Paring knives
For peeling and slicing fruit and vegetables.

POTS AND PANS

Heavy saucepans with lids
Every kitchen needs a couple of saucepans for cooking grains or making sauces or just boiling water.

Nonstick 10-inch pan or skillet
A well-seasoned cast-iron skillet is the way they did nonstick in the old days, and quite frankly, it's still the way I prefer. You can use this pan for cooking on the stove top as well as in the oven. Cooking in a cast-iron skillet adds iron to your diet. Just don't cook with acidic ingredients such as lemon juice, tomatoes, or vinegar in your cast-iron skillet or you'll wind up destroying the pan and getting a horrible, bitter flavor. For acidic recipes, use a conventional nonstick pan or skillet.

Oven-safe casserole
A large (12-inch) Dutch oven or similar casserole that can go from stove top to oven to table seamlessly.

Wok
A well-seasoned or nonstick wok is an endlessly useful piece of equipment. It's the only pan I had in my first two years of college. You can stir-fry, sauté, steam, and make soups in it. Food cooks with much less oil and in a fraction of the time.

BAKING PANS AND BAKING DISHES

Baking sheets (also called cookie sheets or baking trays)
I recommend using heavy-duty aluminum baking sheets. Dark metal sheets, such as nonstick sheets, will brown food more quickly, so if using these, you may need to reduce the temperature by 25°F or shorten your cooking time.

Broiler pan
A broiler pan is essential for quick and easy cooking. You will be using your broiler in heavy rotation, and you need a good pan to put under it.

Rectangular and square baking dishes, ceramic or glass
I mostly use an 11 by 7-inch rectangular and an 8-inch square dish.

Round cake pan, 8-inch, heavy-duty aluminum
For making deep dish pizza.

MISCELLANEOUS COOKING TOOLS

Kitchen timer
Although most modern ovens have a built-in timer, you will sometimes have to keep track of two items at once, so it's a good idea to have a second timer.

Metal spatula
A wide, thin-edged spatula that helps easily transfer hot items from pans.

Microplane (also called a rasp grater or zester)
A stainless steal grater with tiny, razor-sharp teeth that is worth its weight in gold. It's the ultimate tool for zesting citrus and is also perfect for grating chocolate, nutmeg, and ginger.

Mixing bowls
Every kitchen should have a set of mixing bowls, from large to small. Preferably, they should be glass or ceramic, and microwave safe.

Oven mitts and pot holders
While this might seem like a no-brainer, you'd be surprised to learn how many times I've tried transferring hot items from the oven using a folded kitchen towel, only to burn my hands. Invest in the safety of your digits; they're the only ones you've got.

Oven thermometer
Keeping the proper temperature is key to successful results. Being off by more than 5°F or 10°F will alter your final results. Do not depend on your oven's own thermometer, which may be inaccurate: go out and buy yourself an additional one.

Sieve, fine mesh
To strain solids out of liquids.

Silicone spatula
A sturdy silicone spatula will help you transfer items while protecting surfaces from being scratched.

Skewers
A few metal skewers are great to have handy for quick-cooking kebabs and other skewered foods.

Slotted spoon
For transferring foods from liquid that need to drain fast, like fried foods from oil, and gnocchi from water.

Tongs
For turning food in the pan and transferring it.

Vegetable peeler
For peeling potatoes, apples, carrots, and so on.

Whisks, metal and nonstick
It's good to have whisks of varying sizes. I use a large metal whisk to combine dry ingredients, a small metal whisk to combine egg replacer with rice milk, and a medium-size nonstick whisk to whisk things such as pastry custard, pudding, and sauces while they're heating, so as not to scratch the pan.

Wooden spoons
Good wooden spoons will last you a lifetime. You should have a couple for stirring any pot, bowl, or dish that you don't want scratched.

SOUPS
and
STEWS

When we did our first day of shooting for this book, I asked our superlative food stylist, Karen Shinto, what her favorite thing to cook was. After all, she cooks all day, and given the many, many cookbook and magazine photo shoots she's styled, she's probably cooked just about everything. She said, "A roast chicken." Simple. She then asked me the same question. I considered, and answered, "Soup." I know soup is not the most impressive food, but it really is my favorite thing to cook. I like the act of throwing everything into one pot, I like the way it simmers prettily on the stove, I like using a big spoon and a big ladle, it seems old-fashioned and homey and comforting, and quite frankly, I just really love soup. So do my kids, and so does my husband.

If you too are a soup lover, then this chapter is for you. It's got creamy soups, hearty stews, savory chilis, and good old-fashioned chicken noodle soup—all allergy-free and good for the soul.

White Chicken Chili

I've given pretty ample proportions for this chili, because even my eight-year-old goes back for seconds. We like to eat it scooped with tortilla chips. You can adjust the heat to your liking by adding half the jalapeño at first, then more to taste. I also find there is extreme variability in the hotness of jalapeños. Some are super spicy, while others pack no heat, so let your taste guide you here. A great time-saver tip for this recipe is to use your Vidalia Chop Wizard (see page 23), with the larger grid for the onions and bell pepper, and the smaller grid to finely chop the jalapeño in one fell swoop.

SERVES 4 TO 6

1½ pounds chicken tenders
    Salt and freshly ground pepper
3   tablespoons olive oil
1   cup chicken broth
2   (15-ounce) cans cannellini beans
    (white Italian beans), undrained
1   cup diced yellow onion
3   cloves garlic, minced
2   teaspoons ground cumin
1   teaspoon chili powder
1   teaspoon dried oregano
1   jalapeño pepper, stemmed, seeded,
    and finely chopped
1   cup diced green bell pepper
2   teaspoons red wine vinegar
1   tablespoon freshly squeezed lime juice
2   tablespoons minced cilantro
1   ripe avocado, diced
    Shredded Daiya vegan cheddar or pepperjack
    for garnish (optional)
    Lime wedges for garnish (optional)
    Chopped cilantro for garnish (optional)
    Tortilla chips or soft tortillas (optional)

1   Sprinkle the chicken with salt and pepper. Over medium-high heat, set a large, heavy pot or Dutch oven big enough to fit all the tenders in a single layer. Add 2 tablespoons of the olive oil and heat until shimmering and just about to smoke. Add the chicken tenders and cook for 3 minutes. Turn (don't worry if they shred a bit) and cook for 3 minutes more, until golden brown. Transfer to a platter.

2   Meanwhile, combine the chicken broth with one can of the cannellini beans and their liquid in a food processor, and puree.

3   Add the remaining 1 tablespoon olive oil to the Dutch oven and reduce the heat to medium. Add the onion and cook for 2 minutes to soften slightly. Add the garlic and cook for 1 minute more, stirring often.

4   Add the cumin, chili powder, oregano, jalapeño, bell pepper, and ½ teaspoon of salt, and cook for 2 minutes. While the vegetables are cooking, cut the chicken into 1-inch pieces.

5   Add the bean puree and the remaining can of beans and their liquid to the pot, stirring to combine. Bring to a simmer, then deglaze the bottom of the pot, scraping up any browned bits.

Add the red wine vinegar, cover loosely, and cook for 10 minutes, stirring often. Add the chicken, cover loosely, and cook for 5 minutes more over medium-low heat. Remove from the heat and stir in the lime juice and minced cilantro. Serve hot in bowls, topped with chopped avocado, and with the cheese, lime wedges, chopped cilantro, and tortilla chips alongside.

Chipotle Turkey Chili

One of my son Lennon's pet names is "the Chili Monster." He can eat chili three meals a day—and has, many times. He is a child with very specific taste and texture preferences, and so when I find a food he really likes, I jump for joy, and will make it, on demand. Luckily, this version of chili only takes 30 minutes, so when he has a craving, I can just whip up a pot. If you like, you can add one 15-ounce can of corn to the mix, along with the beans, for added carbs and crunch. I prefer it without, by my Chili Monster likes it with, and so that's the way I make it.

SERVES 4 TO 6

2 tablespoons olive oil

1½ cups chopped yellow onion

3 cloves garlic, finely minced or pressed

1 tablespoon plus ½ teaspoon chili powder

¼ teaspoon smoked Spanish paprika

¼ teaspoon ground cumin

⅛ teaspoon ground cinnamon

1½ pounds ground dark meat turkey

¾ cup gluten-free beer

2 (15-ounce) cans fire-roasted diced tomatoes with chipotle chile peppers (or any diced roasted tomatoes with chiles)

1 (15-ounce) can kidney beans, drained and rinsed

1 (15-ounce) can sweet corn (optional)

2 tablespoons brown sugar
Shredded Daiya vegan pepperjack or cheddar for garnish (optional)

1　Heat the olive oil over medium-high heat in a large, heavy pot or Dutch oven. Add the onion and garlic and cook, stirring often, for 3 minutes or until slightly softened.

2　Add the chili powder, paprika, cumin, and cinnamon, and cook 1 minute more, until aromatic.

3　Add the turkey meat and cook, stirring often, for 4 minutes, until the meat is no longer pink and is breaking up into small crumbles. Add the beer and cook for 1 minute more to bring to a simmer.

4　Add the tomatoes, beans, corn, and brown sugar and stir well. Return to a simmer, then reduce the heat to medium-low. Simmer, stirring occasionally, for 20 minutes more. Serve hot, garnished with the vegan cheese.

Cuban Black Beans with Rice and Fried Plantains

Cuban beans usually rely on the flavor boost of a ham hock simmered with the beans for a very long time. I've fast-tracked this recipe by using canned beans and pancetta in place of the ham hock, shaving 90 minutes off the cooking time. Make sure the plantains are ripe—they should have lots of black on the skin.

SERVES 4

1 cup long grain white rice
1½ cups water
1 teaspoon olive oil
Salt
½ cup (3 ounces) diced pancetta
1 cup finely diced yellow onion
2 cloves garlic, minced or pressed
¾ teaspoon dried oregano
1 teaspoon ground cumin
⅛ teaspoon cayenne pepper
1 bay leaf
2 (15-ounce) cans black beans, with liquid
1 teaspoon red wine vinegar
Freshly ground pepper
1 teaspoon brown sugar
2 large ripe plantains
¼ cup canola oil
Kosher salt or coarse sea salt for serving

1 Combine the rice, water, olive oil, and a big pinch of salt in a microwave-safe container. Cover loosely—don't seal. Cook either on the rice sensor setting, or on high for 20 minutes, until all of the water is absorbed. Let rest for 5 minutes, then fluff with a fork.

2 Meanwhile, heat a heavy pot over high heat. Add the pancetta and cook for 3 to 4 minutes, stirring often, until browned. Reduce the heat to medium. Add the onion and cook for 2 minutes, until slightly softened. Add the garlic, oregano, cumin, cayenne, and bay leaf, and cook, stirring, for 1 minute more.

3 Drain one can of the beans and add to the pot. Add the other can with its liquid, along with the red wine vinegar, ¼ teaspoon of salt, a few turns of freshly ground pepper, and the brown sugar. Simmer over medium heat, loosely covered, for 15 minutes, stirring often and scraping up any browned bits on the bottom of the pot. Reduce the heat to medium-low if it's cooking too quickly and you notice burning on the bottom.

4 Meanwhile, slice the plantains into ¼-inch rounds. Heat the canola oil in a large, heavy pan over medium-high heat, until it starts to shimmer but not smoke. Cook the plantains (in batches if necessary so they are not crowded) for 3 minutes per side, until golden brown. Transfer to paper towels. Sprinkle with a little salt and serve alongside the beans and rice.

English Beef Stew

One key to making beef stew in 30 minutes when it's usually a several-hour operation is to get yourself a nice big stew pot or Dutch oven, so you can brown all the beef in one shot. The other trick is to buy an already tender cut of beef. Traditional beef stew is made with tough cuts, like chuck, which take several hours of slow cooking to tenderize. When you don't have the time for that, go for a more tender cut, like top sirloin. Look for sales; sirloin can be as cheap as chuck. If you can find an already chopped mirepoix (prechopped onions, celery, and carrots), just use 3 cups of that for your veggies. Otherwise, use your Vidalia Chop Wizard (see page 23) for speedy prep, or chop the onions, carrots, and celery in the food processor, pulsing until you've got a nice dice.

SERVES 4 TO 6

4	tablespoons olive oil
1½	pounds boneless beef top sirloin, cut into 1-inch cubes (ask the butcher to cube it for you)
12	ounces tiny potatoes (1 inch in diameter) or new potatoes, cut into 1-inch pieces
1	cup diced yellow onion
1	cup diced carrot
1	cup diced celery
2	cloves garlic, minced or pressed
½	teaspoon kosher salt
¼	teaspoon ground pepper
¼	teaspoon smoked Spanish paprika
	Big pinch of ground allspice
3	tablespoons superfine brown rice flour
2½	cups beef broth
2	teaspoons honey
1	tablespoon freshly squeezed lemon juice
¼	cup ketchup

1   Heat 2 tablespoons of the olive oil over high heat in a large heavy pot or casserole (I use a Dutch oven). Once the oil is shimmering and really hot, add the meat, being sure not to overcrowd it, and brown on all sides, 4 to 5 minutes total. Transfer the meat to a plate, tent loosely with aluminum foil, and set aside.

2   Meanwhile, put the potatoes in a microwave-safe container, cover loosely, and microwave on high for 4 minutes. Set aside.

3   Add the remaining 2 tablespoons olive oil to the pot and reduce the heat to medium. Add the onion, carrot, celery, potatoes, garlic, salt, pepper, paprika, and allspice. Cook for 3 minutes, stirring often. Sprinkle over the brown rice flour and cook for 2 minutes more, stirring often.

4   Add the broth, bring to a simmer, and deglaze the pan by scraping up the browned bits at the bottom, about 1 minute. Add the honey, lemon juice, and ketchup. Return to a simmer, reduce the heat to medium-low, and cook for 10 minutes. Return the beef to the pot, heat through, and serve.

Broccoli and Cheddar Soup

For this recipe, I was drawn by the lure of mock cheddar. That's right. Mock cheddar. If you haven't already heard, there's a new kid in town by the name of Daiya, and it's changing the face of dairy-free living. Daiya is a dairy-free, soy-free, vegan cheese product that has revolutionized the way I think about pizza, pasta, and, in this case, cheese soup. Daiya's greatest strength is that it melts, like dairy cheese, a quality that up until now has been virtually impossible with vegan cheeses. I chose to work up an allergy-free broccoli cheddar soup, to see how this new product would perform when it was required not only to melt but also to disappear into the soup completely. Suffice it to say, it rose to the challenge, and then some.

Your special speedy kitchen tool for this recipe is an immersion blender (see page 22). For the broccoli, you can use leftovers or prepare it fresh; combine 3 cups of fresh broccoli with 2 tablespoons of water in a microwave-safe container and microwave, covered, for 2 to 3 minutes, until tender.

SERVES 4

3 tablespoons olive oil
1/4 cup grated yellow onion
3 tablespoons superfine brown rice flour
4 cups chicken broth or vegetable broth
1/4 teaspoon ground white pepper
Pinch of ground nutmeg
1/2 teaspoon salt
Freshly ground pepper
3 cups lightly steamed broccoli florets
2 cups rice milk
1 1/2 cups shredded Daiya vegan cheddar

1   Heat a large, heavy pot over medium-high heat. Add the olive oil and grated onion. Cook, stirring, for about 2 minutes. Add the brown rice flour and cook, stirring, for about 2 minutes more, until lightly golden and aromatic.

2   Add 1 cup of the broth, whisking well to prevent lumps from forming. Add the remaining 3 cups broth, 1 cup at a time, whisking well after each addition.

3   Stir in the white pepper, nutmeg, salt, and a couple of turns of pepper. Bring to a slow boil; reduce to a simmer and cook, stirring often, for about 8 minutes.

4   Chop the broccoli fine and add it to the pot, along with the rice milk. Cook for 10 minutes, until the broccoli is very tender. Then either puree the soup in the pot using a handheld immersion blender or transfer to a blender or food processor to puree (and then return it to the pot).

5   Bring the soup back to a simmer. Add the Daiya cheddar and cook, stirring, until the cheese has completely melted. Serve hot.

Tomato Soup with Grilled Cheese Squares

Tomato soup with grilled cheese is the ultimate comfort food on a cold winter's night. It was my father's staple "warm up the kids" dish when I was a child. It's also a great dish to serve at parties. Pass out mugs of tomato soup and grilled cheese squares for a tasty finger food, perfect for dunking. Make the grilled cheese squares while the soup is simmering. You can find sliced Daiya vegan cheese at the deli counter at Whole Foods.

SERVES 4

2 tablespoons olive oil
1½ cups diced yellow onion
1 clove garlic, minced or pressed
1 teaspoon dried thyme
2 tablespoons superfine brown rice flour
2 cups low-sodium chicken broth or vegetable broth, warmed
¼ teaspoon salt
Freshly ground pepper
1 tablespoon agave nectar
1 (28-ounce) can whole plum tomatoes (preferably San Marzano)
½ cup rice milk

GRILLED CHEESE SQUARES
8 slices allergy-friendly sandwich bread
8 teaspoons Earth Balance soy-free buttery spread, at room temperature
¼ pound thinly sliced Daiya vegan cheddar

1   Heat the olive oil in a large, heavy pot over medium-high-heat. Add the onion and cook for 2 minutes, stirring a few times. Add the garlic and thyme and cook for 1 minute more.

2   Sprinkle in the brown rice flour and cook, stirring, for 2 minutes, until lightly golden and aromatic. Slowly add the warmed broth, stirring. Add the salt and a few turns of pepper and stir in the agave nectar. Reduce the heat to medium and cook for 2 minutes, stirring often. Add the tomatoes, bring to a simmer, reduce the heat to medium-low, and simmer for 10 minutes.

3   Puree in the pot with an immersion blender, or puree in batches in a jar blender or food processor, then return to the pot. Add the rice milk and cook for 5 minutes more. Adjust the salt and pepper to taste.

4   Meanwhile, prepare the grilled cheese squares. Lay out 4 slices of bread. Spread 1 teaspoon of buttery spread on each. Flip so that the buttery side is down. Distribute the vegan cheese evenly among the four sandwiches, and cover each with another slice of bread. Spread 1 teaspoon of buttery spread on top of each.

5   Heat a large nonstick pan or griddle over medium-high heat for 2 minutes. I use a well-seasoned cast-iron pan for this. Add as many sandwiches as will fit, cover, and cook for 2 minutes, until the cheese is starting to melt and the bread is browning on the bottom. Flip the sandwiches and press down hard with a spatula. Cook for about 1 minute more, then flip again and press down to get a final crisp on both sides. Remove the sandwiches from the pan and cut each into quarters. Grill the other sandwiches if you were not able to do them all in one batch. Serve alongside the soup.

Sopa de Lima

Sometimes the challenge of eating allergy-friendly and gluten-free food is all about making smart choices. You begin to look at certain types of cuisine with a fresh eye, because they just might be naturally free of certain allergens. For example, Mexican food relies heavily on the gluten-free grain corn. So it's a pretty safe bet that you can find traditional recipes that are already gluten-free. This lovely Mexican chicken soup comes from the Yucatán, and it is naturally allergy-friendly. If you choose your chicken stock wisely, it's also easily gluten-free. Use your mini chopper to mince the jalapeño, your Vidalia Chop Wizard (see page 23) to chop the onion, and a garlic press for the garlic, and you'll be done with prep, lickety split.

SERVES 4

1 tablespoon olive oil

¾ cup chopped yellow onion

2 large cloves garlic, finely minced or pressed

¼ teaspoon dried oregano (Mexican, if you have it)

½ teaspoon ground cumin

4 black peppercorns
Pinch of ground allspice

4 cups chicken broth

1½ cups diced cooked chicken

1 (14-ounce) can diced tomatoes

1½ teaspoons minced, seeded jalapeño (more if you like more kick)

3 tablespoons freshly squeezed lime juice

1 lime, cut in half lengthwise, then into thin half-moon slices

⅛ teaspoon salt

1 avocado, diced

¼ cup chopped cilantro
Tortilla chips or strips for garnish (see note)
Chopped jalapeños for garnish (optional)

1 Heat the olive oil in a large, heavy pot over medium-high heat. Add the onion and garlic and cook, stirring often, for 2 minutes, until slightly softened.

2 Add the oregano, cumin, peppercorns, and allspice, and cook for 1 minute more.

3 Add the broth and bring to a simmer. Add the chicken, tomatoes, minced jalapeño, lime juice, 1 lime slice, and the salt. Stir, bring to a simmer, reduce the heat to medium-low, and cook for about 15 minutes.

4 To serve, ladle soup into bowls, top with avocado, a couple slices of lime, cilantro, and tortilla chips. Add a little more chopped jalapeño if you like it spicy.

* Note: To make tortilla strips, slice 4 ounces of fresh corn tortillas into ¼-inch strips. Pour canola or safflower oil into a large sauté pan so it is ½ inch deep, then heat over high heat until starting to shimmer. Drop the tortilla strips into the pan and cook until deeply golden and slightly puffed, about 1 to 2 minutes. Remove with a slotted spoon or spatula and drain on paper towels.

Hearty Italian Soup

This soup is quick and easy—a complete meal, all in one pot. The easiest way to remove sausage meat from Italian sausages is to gently slice them vertically down one side, then peel back the casing, popping out the sausage.

SERVES 4

4   ounces hot Italian sausage
4   ounces sweet Italian sausage
3   cloves garlic, finely minced or pressed
2   teaspoons dried oregano
2   cups low-sodium chicken broth
2   (14.5-ounce) cans roasted diced tomatoes
    Freshly ground pepper
½   cup spiral brown rice pasta
3   cups baby spinach or chard
2   tablespoons chopped fresh basil
4   tablespoons shredded Daiya vegan mozzarella

1   Remove the sausage from its casings. Heat a large pot over medium heat. Add the sausage and garlic and cook, stirring and using a wooden spoon to break up the sausage, until browned and crumbly, about 5 minutes. Add the oregano and cook 1 minute more.

2   Add the chicken broth, diced tomatoes, a few turns of pepper, and the pasta. Bring to a boil over high heat. Cover loosely, reduce the heat, and cook at a simmer until the pasta is tender, about 15 minutes. Add the spinach and cook a minute or so more, until it's wilted.

3   Ladle the soup into bowls and serve garnished with a little chopped basil and a tablespoon of the mozzarella.

Chicken Noodle Soup

Buy prechopped veggies and rotisserie chicken to express-lane this dish. Look for the plain unseasoned rotisserie chicken, or just use any leftover cooked chicken you have—it's all good! I prefer Tinkyada spirals or Lundberg brown rice rotini for this soup, because they hold their shape best. Avoid the Tinkyada fusilli, which tend to swell up into huge noodles and take over your soup pot.

SERVES 4

6 cups low-sodium chicken broth

1 tablespoon olive oil

1 cup diced yellow onion

1 cup diced celery

$1/2$ cup diced carrot

$1/2$ teaspoon dried thyme

Salt and freshly ground pepper

2 cups hot water

2 cups gluten-free spiral pasta

2 cups shredded or diced cooked boneless, skinless chicken

1 tablespoon chopped fresh parsley

1   Pour the broth into a microwave-safe container and heat for 4 minutes on high until piping hot.

2   Meanwhile, heat the olive oil over medium-high heat in a heavy pot. Add the onion, celery, carrot, and thyme. Cook for 3 minutes, stirring often, until slightly softened.

3   Add $1/2$ teaspoon of salt and a few turns of pepper to the vegetables. Pour in the hot broth and hot water. Bring to a boil, add the pasta, and cook for 7 minutes, or until al dente. Add the chicken and parsley and cook for 3 minutes more. Adjust the salt and pepper to taste. Serve piping hot.

Vietnamese Beef Noodle Soup

How to make pho without fish sauce? I pondered the question for a while. Salty, sweet, tangy, and sour all needed to be replicated, along with umami, that earthy depth of flavor. I settled on a combination of lime juice and lemon juice (tangy and sour), the Japanese rice wine mirin (sweet and salty), sugar (sweet), salt (salty, of course), and then ginger, garlic, and Chinese five-spice powder for that depth of flavor. Delicious! The fresh herbs bring it all together. Serve with extra chiles or chile sauce on the side if you like it really hot (which I do).

SERVES 4

3¹/₂ cups beef broth

3¹/₂ cups low-sodium chicken broth

1 (3-inch) piece ginger, skin on, sliced into thin rounds

3 cloves garlic, thinly sliced

1 shallot, thinly sliced

1¹/₂ teaspoons Chinese five-spice powder

Salt

1 tablespoon sugar

2 tablespoons freshly squeezed lime juice

1 tablespoon freshly squeezed lemon juice

1 tablespoon mirin

8 ounces ¹/₈- to ¹/₄-inch-wide rice noodles

3 green onions, white and green parts, chopped

¹/₃ cup chopped cilantro

¹/₃ cup coarsely chopped basil

12 ounces center-cut beef tenderloin, halved and very thinly sliced crosswise (or use leftover steak, very thinly sliced into bite-size pieces)

1 cup mung bean sprouts

1 lime, cut into 8 wedges

2 to 4 Thai or serrano chiles, or use chile paste or chile sauce, like Sriracha

1 In a large pot over medium-high heat, combine the beef broth, chicken broth, ginger, garlic, shallot, and five-spice powder. Bring to a boil, and then reduce to a simmer over medium-low-heat. Add ¹/₂ teaspoon of salt and the sugar, lime juice, lemon juice, and mirin. Simmer uncovered for 20 minutes.

2 Meanwhile, bring a large pot of water to a boil, and cook the noodles according to the instructions on the package. Drain and rinse the noodles and divide them evenly among 4 bowls. Divide the green onions and herbs evenly among the bowls. Top with the thinly sliced steak.

3 Strain the broth through a strainer or fine-mesh sieve. Pour the broth, still boiling hot, over the steak, about 1¹/₂ cups per bowl. The hot broth will cook the thinly sliced steak. Top with the bean sprouts, a couple of wedges of lime, and chiles according to your heat preference. Sprinkle with salt.

PASTA
and
NOODLES

I call my son Monte a chickpea, but if the old adage "You are what you eat" is true, my son Lennon is definitely some type of pasta. He can eat pasta three meals a day with pleasure. He is a carb loader. Given his somewhat peckish appetite, I go with what works a lot of the time. And besides, carbs are brain fuel. So we eat a lot of pasta: the truth is out.

In this chapter, I'll teach you how to make a cheese-free creamy mac 'n' cheese; spaghetti and meatballs with chunky marinara sauce; gluten-, dairy-, and nut-free pesto; fettuccine alfredo; penne chicken Marsala; and that old-time cafeteria favorite, chili mac. Pasta is so hearty, so easy, so kid-friendly, and best of all, it's cheap! And that, my friends, is a great thing indeed.

Please note that pasta cooking time varies by brand; Ancient Harvest usually takes a minute or so longer than the package instructions specify, and Tinkyada generally cooks faster than it says on the package. To be safe, test for doneness as you go.

Chili Mac

My son Monte helped in the development of this recipe. It's true kid food that grown-ups love too, because of nostalgia—I used to be served this for lunch in my elementary school cafeteria. So I used Monte's age to my advantage. He was my prep cook and taster. He measured out the water, opened the tomato sauce, measured and mixed the cheeses, and sampled as we went along. When it was finished, and we both declared it yummy, he smiled and said, "You and I have the same palate, Mom." Yes, he really said that. It also happens to be my son Lennon's favorite recipe in this book. I like to use Quinoa Corporation's Ancient Harvest gluten-free elbow macaroni for this recipe.

SERVES 6

1 tablespoon plus 1½ teaspoons olive oil

1 cup diced yellow onion

2 cloves garlic, minced or pressed

1 tablespoon chili powder

¼ teaspoon smoked Spanish paprika

1 teaspoon ground cumin

1 pound ground beef, bison, or dark meat turkey

1 tablespoon brown sugar

Salt

2 cups water

1 (15-ounce) can tomato sauce

8 ounces gluten-free elbow macaroni

⅔ cup shredded Daiya vegan pepperjack

⅔ cup shredded Daiya vegan cheddar

⅔ cup shredded Daiya vegan mozzarella

Freshly ground pepper

1   Preheat the broiler on high.

2   Heat the olive oil over medium heat in a large, heavy, oven-safe pan. Add the onion and garlic and cook, stirring often, for 2 minutes, until slightly softened.

3   Add the spices and cook, stirring, for 1 minute more, until aromatic.

4   Add the meat and cook, stirring often, for 4 minutes or until no longer pink, breaking it up into a small crumble. Sprinkle with the brown sugar and ¼ teaspoon of salt, stir, and cook for 1 minute more.

5   Add the water and tomato sauce, increase the heat to medium-high, add the pasta, and stir well. Bring to a simmer, then reduce the heat to medium again. Simmer, stirring often, for 10 minutes or until the pasta is al dente. Meanwhile, toss together the three cheeses. Add 1 cup of the cheese mixture to the pasta. Stir, and season with salt and pepper to taste. Stir well. Top with the remaining cup of cheese. Broil 6 inches from the heat source for about 5 minutes, until the cheese has melted and is just starting to brown. Watch carefully so they don't burn. Let rest for a few minutes—this puppy is hot!

Creamy Mac 'n' Cheese

We all know mac 'n' cheese is the ultimate American comfort food. And it's no secret that homemade mac 'n' cheese is much better than the boxed or frozen stuff. In this recipe, I'll teach you how to make a dairy-free, gluten-free roux. A roux is the basis of a cream sauce, which is essential to giving mac 'n' cheese that coveted creaminess. Adding Daiya vegan cheddar cheese turns the cream sauce into a cheese sauce, and you've got yourself a classic American staple. Tinkyada brown rice penne is my favorite for this recipe.

SERVES 4

6 ounces brown rice penne
1 cup rice milk
2 tablespoons olive oil
1 tablespoon grated yellow onion
2 tablespoons superfine brown rice flour
1 bay leaf
Pinch of cayenne pepper
Pinch of white pepper
Pinch of ground nutmeg
1/4 teaspoon salt
1 1/2 teaspoons Dijon mustard
Freshly ground pepper
1 1/2 cups shredded Daiya vegan cheddar

1   Bring a large pot of water to a boil and cook the pasta according to the package instructions, until tender. Drain and set aside.

2   Preheat the broiler on high.

3   Once the pasta is cooking, scald the rice milk—heat it in a saucepan until hot but not boiling. Set aside.

4   Heat the olive oil over medium heat in a heavy saucepan. Add the onion and cook, stirring often, for 2 minutes. Add the brown rice flour and cook, stirring, for 2 minutes more, until golden. Don't burn it, and don't worry if it clumps a bit. This is your roux.

5   Add the rice milk a little at a time, whisking continuously and vigorously until smooth. Add the bay leaf, a big pinch of cayenne, and the white pepper and nutmeg. Add the salt and mustard, stir, and bring to a simmer. Reduce the heat to low and cook, stirring, until thick and creamy, about 4 minutes. Whisk again to smooth if necessary. Add a few turns of pepper. Add 1 cup of the vegan cheddar and stir until melted, about 4 minutes. Remove from the heat.

6   Add the pasta to the cheese sauce and stir to combine.

7   Drizzle a little olive oil in the bottom of an 8 by 8-inch baking dish. Pour in the pasta. Top with the remaining 1/2 cup vegan cheddar. Put under the broiler for 5 minutes, until the cheese has melted and is browning up a bit. Remove from the oven, and let rest for 10 minutes before serving.

Homemade Gnocchi

I spent a lot of time on this recipe, trying to shave off minutes. The way I used to make gnocchi when time was of no importance was to boil the potatoes whole, in their skins. When I switched to quicker methods, the dough no longer behaved. I tried cooking the potatoes in the microwave and then peeling off their skins, but they were too dry and crumbly when it came time to roll out the dough. I used varying methods of mashing the potatoes, thinking that might be the solution, but to no avail. I used different types of potatoes, thinking it must have to do with different starch levels, but that didn't help either, and finally, I determined that the potatoes really needed to be boiled, after all. And so, ultimately, I decided to peel and dice the potatoes and boil them in the microwave. It worked! Traditional recipes also call for using a potato ricer, but I don't have one, so I use an electric handheld mixer, and it works fine. If you have a potato ricer, by all means go ahead and use it.

Please note that these gnocchi keep very nicely after cooking, drizzled with a little olive oil and tightly covered in the fridge, so feel free to make them several hours or a day in advance and reheat lightly in the microwave before serving. You may also make the gnocchi and refrigerate them for a couple of days, cooking them when you're ready. Serve them hot with your favorite sauce; I love them with just a little olive oil and truffle salt. Although truffle salt may sound exotic, it's easy to find and is a really simple way to add a ton of flavor with just a tiny pinch. It may become one of your most frequently used ingredients (see Resources).

SERVES 4

12 ounces Yukon Gold potatoes
     Salt
1   teaspoon canola oil
3/4 cup Authentic Foods GF Classical Blend or Basic
     Gluten-Free Flour Mix (recipe follows)
3/4 teaspoon xanthan gum
3   tablespoons rice milk
1   tablespoon plus 1 1/2 teaspoons olive oil,
     plus more for drizzling

1   Peel the potatoes, cut them into 1- to 2-inch pieces, and put in a microwave-safe bowl; cover with water, making sure the water comes up a couple of inches above the potatoes. Add 1/4 teaspoon salt and the canola oil (this keeps the potatoes from boiling over). Cook in the microwave for about 12 minutes, stopping to test for tenderness with a fork halfway through. Once fork-tender, drain.

2   Bring a large pot of water to a boil.

3   Combine the flour mix with the xanthan gum.

4   Put the potatoes in a bowl and combine with the rice milk, olive oil, and 1/8 teaspoon salt, beating with an electric mixer until light and fluffy.

5   Turn the potatoes out onto a work surface. You want them still warm; if they aren't, give them a minute or so in the microwave.

. . . continued

6   Sprinkle the potatoes with half the flour mixture and use your hands to knead it in. Add the remaining flour and knead the dough until it's smooth but still slightly sticky. Mold into a ball. Divide into three balls. Roll each ball out into a sausage-shaped log, about 1 inch in diameter. Cut the logs into $1/2$-inch-thick rounds.

7   Using a fork, with the front side facing you, press the gnocchi into the base of the fork, using your thumb to make an indentation. Then use your index finger to flip the gnocchi toward the handle, which helps curl the gnocchi slightly. Let the gnocchi fall onto your work surface. (The post for Allergy-Free Gnocchi on www.cybelepascal.com has step-by-step photos.) Repeat with the remaining gnocchi. Making them in this fashion, with grooves on one side and a cupped shape on the other, allows the sauce to cling to them better. I find I have to switch forks a few times, because the fork tines get sticky after a while, and a clean fork surface works best.

8   Once you've made all your gnocchi, add a large pinch of salt to the boiling water. You will cook the gnocchi in several batches. Add the first batch of gnocchi to the water, being careful not to overcrowd them, and cook until they bob to the surface. Once they've bobbed up, cook for 10 seconds longer, then remove from the water with a slotted spoon and put them in a bowl drizzled with a little olive oil. Do not overcook them! Cover to keep warm while cooking the remaining gnocchi. Serve hot.

BASIC GLUTEN-FREE FLOUR MIX

4   cups superfine brown rice flour
$1^1/_3$ cups potato starch (not potato flour)
$2/_3$ cup tapioca flour (also called tapioca starch)

1   To measure flour, use a large spoon to scoop flour into the measuring cup, then level it off with the back of a knife or straightedge. Do not use the measuring cup itself to scoop your flour when measuring! It will compact the flour and you will wind up with too much for the recipe.

2   Combine all ingredients in a gallon-size zipper-top bag. Shake until well blended. Store in the refrigerator until ready to use.

Penne Chicken Marsala

How many times in your life have you made chicken Marsala and pasta? I know I've done it dozens of times. But then it finally occurred to me, why make two dishes when you can make one? This version saves on time, and cuts down on dishes to wash later.

SERVES 4 TO 6

1½ pounds chicken tenders, halved
   Salt and freshly ground pepper
⅓ cup superfine brown rice flour
5 tablespoons olive oil
6 tablespoons diced prosciutto
   (about 2½ ounces)
10 ounces sliced button mushrooms
2 large cloves garlic, finely minced or pressed
¾ cup sweet Marsala
½ cup low-sodium chicken broth
12 ounces gluten-free penne
   Minced fresh parsley
   Shredded Daiya vegan mozzarella (optional)

1   Pat the chicken tenders dry and sprinkle them with salt and pepper. Put the brown rice flour in a shallow dish. Turn the chicken in the flour to coat and set aside.

2   Bring a pot of water to a boil for the pasta.

3   Heat 2 tablespoons of the olive oil over medium-high heat, until starting to ripple. Add the prosciutto and cook for 2 minutes, stirring often, until it's starting to crisp up a bit.

4   Add the mushrooms and garlic and cook, stirring often, for 8 minutes or until the mushrooms have released most of their juices and are starting to brown up. Transfer the contents of the pan to a bowl and set aside.

5   Add 2 more tablespoons of the olive oil to the pan and heat until almost smoking. Add half of the chicken and cook for 2 minutes per side, until golden brown and cooked through. Transfer to the bowl with the mushrooms. Add the remaining 1 tablespoon olive oil to the pan and cook the rest of the chicken until golden brown and cooked through. Transfer to the bowl with the mushrooms.

6   Add the Marsala and broth to the pan, bring to a simmer, reduce the heat to medium, and deglaze, scraping up all the little browned bits along the bottom with a wooden spoon. Cook to reduce slightly, about 3 minutes.

7   Add the chicken and mushrooms back to the pan with the sauce. Cook over medium-low heat for 7 minutes, until the chicken is warmed through and the sauce has thickened up a bit.

8   Meanwhile, cook the pasta according to the instructions on the package.

9   Drain the pasta, toss with the chicken and mushrooms and sauce, and serve sprinkled with a little minced parsley and vegan mozzarella.

Spaghetti and Meatballs with Quick Chunky Marinara Sauce

The food processor will once again be your best friend while you're making this classic favorite. Use the shredder attachment to grate your onion in about ten seconds; pulse 1½ cups of cornflakes with the blade attachment to yield the ½ cup of crumbs you'll need for the meatballs. If you don't have a Vidalia Chop Wizard (see page 23), you can also use the food processor to finely dice your red onion, by pulsing it with the blade attachment.

SERVES 6

MEATBALLS

- ½ cup cornflake crumbs or gluten-free breadcrumbs
- ⅓ cup plain vegan yogurt
- ½ cup grated yellow onion
- 2 cloves garlic, minced or pressed
- 1½ pounds ground dark turkey meat
- 1 teaspoon dried oregano
- 1 teaspoon salt
- ¼ teaspoon pepper
- ¼ cup chopped fresh parsley
- ¼ cup olive oil

QUICK CHUNKY MARINARA SAUCE

- 1 tablespoon olive oil
- 1 cup finely diced red onion
- 3 cloves garlic, minced or pressed
- ¾ teaspoon dried oregano
- 1 (28-ounce) can whole plum tomatoes (preferably San Marzano)
  Freshly ground pepper
- ¼ teaspoon salt
- 2 teaspoons balsamic vinegar

- 1 pound gluten-free spaghetti
  Olive oil

1 To make the meatballs, combine the cornflake crumbs with the yogurt in a bowl and stir until it forms a paste.

2 Combine the grated onion, garlic, turkey meat, oregano, salt, pepper, chopped parsley, and crumb yogurt paste in the bowl of a stand mixer fitted with the paddle attachment. Mix on medium speed until combined, about 1 minute. Break up any crumb clumps. Use a 2-tablespoon cookie scoop to make about 24 balls, rolling each ball smooth with your hands. Set the meatballs aside on a large plate as you form them.

3 Heat the ¼ cup olive oil in a large heavy casserole or Dutch oven over medium-high heat. Make sure the pan is really hot before adding the meatballs, or they'll stick. Cook the meatballs for 5 to 6 minutes, until browned on all sides, shaking the pan after the first 2 minutes (but not before, or they'll break up!). Transfer to a bowl or plate and set aside.

. . . continued

4   To make the sauce, return the pan to the stove over medium heat. Add the 1 tablespoon olive oil and the onion, garlic, and oregano, and cook for 2 to 3 minutes, until the onion is tender, stirring often. Add the tomatoes with their juice and crush with a potato masher or the back of a fork. Add the meatballs back in, along with a few turns of pepper and a big pinch of salt. Cook for 5 minutes. Add the balsamic vinegar and cook for 10 minutes more, stirring occasionally.

5   Meanwhile, cook the spaghetti according to the instructions on the package. Drain the pasta and toss with a little olive oil to coat. Divide the pasta among 6 bowls and ladle the sauce and meatballs over the top.

Fettuccine Alfredo with Bacon

Miraculously, with the advent of Daiya vegan cheeses—and a few tricks of allergy-free alchemy—you can still have this classic creamy Italian favorite. Brown rice flour, rice milk, and a little chicken broth make the "cream" sauce, and bacon stands in for the butter. I also really love this with Ancient Harvest corn/quinoa linguine, which has a slightly golden hue. If you have access to truffles or truffle salt, add a little when you serve, for perfection in a bowl.

SERVES 4

8 ounces gluten-free fettuccine or linguine
4 slices thick-cut bacon, cut crosswise into ½-inch pieces
2 cloves garlic, finely minced or pressed
1 tablespoon superfine brown rice flour
1 cup rice milk, warmed, plus up to ½ cup more
⅔ cup shredded Daiya vegan mozzarella
¼ teaspoon salt
   Pinch of ground nutmeg
¼ cup low-sodium chicken broth, warmed
   Freshly ground pepper

1   Bring a large pot of water to a boil over high heat. Cook the pasta according to the instructions on the package. Drain and set aside.

2   Meanwhile, cook the bacon in a large nonstick skillet (I use cast-iron) over medium-high heat, stirring a few times, until crispy, about 4 minutes. Remove the pan from the heat, reduce the temperature to low, and use a slotted spoon to transfer the bacon to paper towels to drain. Set aside for later.

3   Pour off half the bacon fat and return the pan to low heat. Add the garlic and cook, stirring, for 20 seconds or until just starting to turn golden. Sprinkle in the brown rice flour and cook, stirring, for 1 minute or until golden and aromatic. Add 1 cup of the warm rice milk, increase the heat to medium low, and cook at a simmer, stirring, for about 2 minutes, until starting to thicken slightly. Add the vegan mozzarella, salt, and nutmeg. Cook, stirring often, until the cheese melts, about 3 minutes. Stir in the warm chicken broth and a few turns of pepper. Cook for a minute or so more, until the sauce is thick and creamy, adding a little more warm rice milk if it gets too thick.

4   Add the drained pasta to the pan and toss well, adding half of the bacon and a few more turns of pepper. Serve warm, sprinkled with the remaining bacon.

Penne with Hemp Seed Pesto and Roasted Cherry Tomatoes

Summer is the season for tomatoes and basil! But pesto is usually off-limits for people with food allergies—it traditionally contains tree nuts and dairy—so I set about creating an allergy-free version. The sweet and tangy roasted cherry tomatoes are the perfect complement to the earthy flavor of the basil. As a bonus, I've used hemp seeds in place of the usual pine nuts or walnuts, boosting protein and omega-3 essential fatty acids. Upon tasting this recipe, my son Monte asked, "Can I have this for lunch tomorrow, too?" There is no greater compliment.

If you wish, add 12 ounces of cubed grilled chicken breast. Trader Joe's sells sliced grilled chicken that is actually quite tasty, and heats up in just a minute or so, in either a stove-top grill pan or the microwave. I like Hol-Grain gluten-free breadcrumbs for this recipe—they're made from rice and are very fine. You'll have about 1 heaping cup of pesto.

SERVES 4

8   ounces cherry tomatoes
1   tablespoon extra virgin olive oil, plus extra
    for coating
    Salt and freshly ground pepper
8   ounces gluten-free penne, spirals, or shells

HEMP SEED PESTO

3   tablespoons shelled hemp seeds
1   small clove garlic
½   cup tightly packed fresh basil
6   tablespoons extra virgin olive oil
⅛   teaspoon salt
2   tablespoons gluten-free breadcrumbs

4   large basil leaves for garnish

1   Preheat the oven to 425°F. Cover a baking tray with aluminum foil, scatter the tomatoes on it, drizzle with the 1 tablespoon extra virgin olive oil, sprinkle with salt and pepper, and toss until all the tomatoes are coated. Roast until the tomatoes collapse in on themselves, about 25 minutes (it will be less if the tomatoes are really tiny).

2   Meanwhile, bring a large pot of water to a boil and cook the pasta according to the instructions on the package.

3   To make the pesto, put the hemp seeds in a food processor and grind to a fine meal. Add the garlic and puree, then add the basil and blend until it's finely chopped, scraping down the sides of the bowl with a rubber spatula as necessary. Pour in the extra virgin olive oil a little at a time until the pesto is nice and smooth. Add the salt and the gluten-free breadcrumbs. Combine thoroughly and set aside.

4   Drain the pasta and toss with a little more olive oil to coat in a large pasta bowl. Add the pesto and toss, then add the roasted tomatoes and gently toss one more time. Scatter the basil leaves over the top and serve.

Linguine Vesuvio

This dish is named linguine Vesuvio because it was created to look like the volcano (Mount Vesuvius) erupting into streams of molten lava. Ask for the sliced Daiya vegan mozzarella at the deli counter at Whole Foods; have them slice it thick so you can cube it. If you can eat dairy, use fresh mozzarella instead. For the pasta, I'm partial to Ancient Harvest linguine, made with a corn/quinoa blend.

SERVES 4

1   (28-ounce) can whole plum tomatoes (preferably San Marzano)

2   tablespoons olive oil, plus more for drizzling

2   cloves garlic, finely minced or pressed

1   teaspoon dried oregano

¼   cup shredded Daiya vegan mozzarella
    Big pinch of salt

8   ounces gluten-free linguine

4   ounces thick-sliced Daiya vegan mozzarella

1   Combine the tomatoes and olive oil in a pot. Use a fork to squash and mash the tomatoes. Add the garlic, oregano, shredded vegan mozzarella, and salt. Bring to a simmer over medium heat and cook rapidly for 20 minutes, stirring often, until rich and slightly creamy.

2   Meanwhile, bring a large pot of water to a boil and cook the pasta according to the instructions on the package. While it's cooking, chop the sliced vegan mozzarella into ½-inch cubes.

3   Drain the pasta. Drizzle a little olive oil into the bottom of a serving bowl and add the pasta, sauce, and cubes of mozzarella. Toss. Cover for 5 minutes, so that the mozzarella begins to melt and look like molten lava. Serve hot.

SunButter Dan Dan Noodles

When my kids were very small, we lived in Westchester County, New York. My husband and I used to go on date night to a Chinese restaurant in Yonkers called Hunan Village. It was owned by a regal Chinese man named Paul. He was the most impressive host. He liked to order for our table, and it was thanks to him that I first tried dan dan noodles. I've eaten them many times at restaurants since, and none compares to the ones at Hunan Village. They had the best darn dan dan noodles I've ever tasted. Funny thing about that restaurant was my husband had been going to it ever since he was a kid, and Paul was the owner, all the way back then. I've heard Paul left Hunan Village a few years ago, and that sadly their food has declined. In honor of Paul, I devised this scrumptious, addictive, allergy-friendly dan dan noodle recipe, because the traditional is chock-full of allergens (wheat, soy, peanuts). I hope my version does justice to Paul. For the linguine, I like corn-quinoa noodles that mimic the yellow hue of the traditional egg noodles.

SERVES 4

8 ounces gluten-free linguine

2 cloves garlic, finely minced or pressed

2 tablespoons finely minced or grated ginger

2 tablespoons coconut amino acids

2 tablespoons canola oil

1 tablespoon dark brown sugar

1 tablespoon balsamic vinegar

1 tablespoon Sriracha or Thai Chile Sauce (page 94)

1/3 cup smooth SunButter

1/4 cup low-sodium chicken broth or vegetable broth

1/2 teaspoon salt

3 green onions, white and green parts, chopped

1 tablespoon chopped cilantro

1/4 cup roasted sunflower seeds, plus more for garnish

1/2 English cucumber, peeled, quartered, and diced, for garnish

1   Bring a large pot of water to a boil over high heat. Cook the pasta according to the instructions on the package.

2   In a large bowl, combine the garlic, ginger, coconut amino acids, oil, sugar, vinegar, and chile sauce. Mix well. Add the SunButter, chicken broth, and salt, and stir until smooth.

3   Drain the pasta and combine with the sauce, tossing to coat. Mix in the green onions, cilantro, and 1/4 cup sunflower seeds.

4   Serve garnished with the diced cucumber and a sprinkling of sunflower seeds.

Thai Noodle Salad with Chicken

Thai food is usually loaded with common allergens—from the fish sauce to the soy sauce to the chopped peanuts that are so often the finishing touch. Here, I've created an allergy-free noodle salad to satisfy that Thai food craving. Buy shredded cabbage (for coleslaw), shredded carrots, and precut bell peppers to fast-track the prep.

SERVES 4

4 ounces rice noodles (pad Thai or maifun)

1 cup shredded cabbage

½ cup shredded carrot

¼ English cucumber, quartered and diced

½ cup red or yellow bell pepper strips, halved

1 cup cubed cooked chicken breast

2 green onions, white and green parts, chopped

2 tablespoons chopped fresh basil

2 tablespoons chopped fresh mint

½ teaspoon salt

2 tablespoons plus 1 teaspoon freshly squeezed lime juice

4 teaspoons rice vinegar

1 tablespoon light agave nectar

1 tablespoon mirin

2 teaspoons Sriracha or Thai Chile Sauce (page 94)

2 tablespoons canola oil

Fresh mint leaves for garnish

1 Bring a large pot of water to a boil over high heat. Boil the noodles according to the instructions on the package. Place the cabbage in a colander and drain the noodles over the cabbage. Rinse with cold water, and drain.

2 Toss the cabbage and noodles in a large bowl with the carrot, cucumber, bell pepper, chicken, green onions, basil, and mint. Use your hands or tongs, whichever you find easiest. Sprinkle with the salt, and toss well.

3 In a separate bowl, whisk together the lime juice, rice vinegar, agave nectar, mirin, chile sauce, and canola oil. Pour over the noodles and toss. Adjust the salt to taste. Garnish with a few whole mint leaves.

Pasta Salad

A good pasta salad is all about proportions and the right amount of savory oomph. I like my pasta salad more Mediterranean than Asian-inspired, so I bump it up with marinated artichoke hearts, capers, and olives. The creamy vinaigrette with a little lemon zest brings it all together. Great for picnics, summer suppers, or any old time, this salad can be made with chicken, or use chickpeas for a vegan option. For extra greens, try mixing in a little baby arugula.

SERVES 4

8 ounces short gluten-free pasta

½ cup marinated artichoke hearts, quartered

¼ cup diced red bell pepper

¼ cup sliced black olives

½ cup fresh sliced mushrooms

1 tablespoon capers, drained

½ cup finely minced yellow or red onion

1 cup diced cooked chicken or chickpeas, drained and rinsed

⅓ cup diced tomatoes

1 tablespoon chopped fresh basil

2 tablespoons chopped fresh parsley
Salt and freshly ground pepper

1 clove garlic, finely minced, pressed, or smashed

2 tablespoons rice vinegar

1 tablespoon Dijon mustard, vegan soy-free mayonnaise (see Resources), or Rice Milk Mayonnaise (page 135)

⅓ cup extra virgin olive oil

½ teaspoon freshly grated lemon zest

1   Bring a large pot of salted water to a boil over high heat. Cook the pasta according to the instructions on the package, being sure not to overcook it. Drain the pasta, but don't rinse it. Pour it out onto a baking tray and let it cool.

2   Combine the artichoke hearts, bell pepper, olives, mushrooms, and capers in a large bowl. Gently toss in the onion. Add the chicken and tomatoes and toss. Sprinkle in the basil and parsley and season with salt and pepper.

3   In a small bowl, combine the garlic, rice vinegar, mustard, and a little salt and pepper. Slowly drizzle in the extra virgin olive oil, whisking, until you have a creamy emulsion. Whisk in the lemon zest.

4   Combine the pasta and the artichoke and chicken mixture, pour in the dressing, toss, and adjust the salt and pepper to taste. Serve at room temperature or chilled.

CASSEROLES
and
POTPIES

One-pot meals are the ultimate free 'n' easy. Everything cooks in one dish, saving you time on prep as well as cleanup. That's one reason casserole cooking is so popular. The other is that it's really inviting to put an oven-to-table baking dish, steaming hot and heavenly smelling, like it's out of a Norman Rockwell painting, in the center of your table.

These casseroles, from the chicken noodle casserole to the paella to the shepherd's pie, are all usually heavily dependent on the top eight allergens. But there was no way I was going to let my family or yours miss out on traditional comfort foods. So I used a little ingenuity and came up with my own version of Campbell's cream of mushroom soup for the noodle casserole, subbed chicken for tuna, and figured out how to make a roux and biscuits for a creamy chicken potpie. One more great thing: if you have leftovers, just cover that casserole, stick it in the fridge, and rewarm it the next day. Two meals in one never sounded better!

Shepherd's Pie

I really didn't know it was possible to whip up a shepherd's pie in less than half an hour until I set my mind to it. I have had so much fun working on these recipes, partly because they're delicious, but also because they've simplified my life so dramatically by cutting my time not only in half, but often by two-thirds or more. I actually prefer this shepherd's pie to the slow-cooked one I used to make. The big trick? Microwaving potatoes cuts your mashed potato making time in half. There are a few other tricks that you'll need to read on to gather.

Another great benefit of this casserole is that it's a lot lower in fat than traditional shepherd's pie, but really not missing out on any of the rich flavor.

SERVES 4 TO 6

POTATO TOPPING

- 2 pounds russet potatoes or other baking potatoes
- 2 tablespoons plain vegan yogurt
- 2 tablespoons olive oil
- 1/4 teaspoon salt
- 1/4 cup rice milk

FILLING

- 2 tablespoons olive oil
- 1 cup diced yellow onion
- 1 cup diced carrot
- 1/2 cup diced celery
- 1 pound 90 percent lean ground bison or beef
  Salt and freshly ground pepper
  Big pinch of ground cloves
- 2 tablespoons superfine brown rice flour
- 3/4 cup beef broth
- 2 tablespoons ketchup
- 1 tablespoon Pickapeppa Sauce, or 1 teaspoon ketchup plus a splash of Tabasco
- 1 tablespoon Earth Balance soy-free buttery spread or olive oil
  Sweet paprika

1   To make the topping, prick the potatoes a few times with a fork, put in a microwave-safe dish, cover, and cook in the microwave for 10 to 12 minutes, until tender (or if you have a baked potato setting, use that). Let the potatoes rest for 5 minutes in the microwave. Remove, split in half, and spoon out the potatoes' flesh. They will be hot, so use a kitchen towel or gloves to protect your hands.

2   Using an electric hand mixer, whip together the potato, yogurt, olive oil, salt, and rice milk. Whip until fluffy. Set aside.

3   Preheat the broiler on high.

4   To make the filling, heat the olive oil in a large heavy pan or Dutch oven over medium-high heat. Once the oil starts to shimmer, add the onion, carrot, celery, and ground meat. Break up the meat with a wooden spoon. Sprinkle with salt and pepper and the cloves. Cook, stirring often, for 5 minutes, until the meat is no longer pink.

. . . continued

5   Sprinkle the meat and vegetables with the brown rice flour, reduce the heat to medium, and cook for 2 minutes, stirring often.

6   Add the beef broth, bring to a boil, and use a wooden spoon or spatula to deglaze the bottom of the pan, scraping up any browned bits, about 1 minute. Add the ketchup and Pickapeppa Sauce and cook, stirring, for 1 minute.

7   Transfer the meat and vegetables to a 7 by 11-inch casserole or baking dish. Top evenly with mashed potatoes, dot the top with the buttery spread, and sprinkle with the paprika.

8   Broil 6 inches from the heat source for 6 to 8 minutes, until the top is browned. Keep a close eye on it so it doesn't burn.

Tex-Mex Casserole

This is sort of like Tex-Mex lasagna, except that it takes way less time than lasagna does. The combo of Daiya vegan cheddar, pepperjack, and mozzarella is just like Mexican shredded cheese, and makes for a pretty finish.

SERVES 6

6 large handfuls tortilla chips (about 50 chips)
2 tablespoons olive oil
1 cup diced yellow onion
2 cloves garlic, minced or pressed
2 teaspoons chili powder
1 teaspoon ground cumin
1 pound ground dark meat turkey
  Salt and freshly ground pepper
1 (15-ounce) can pinto beans, drained
  Juice of 1 lime
1 (15-ounce) can diced roasted tomatoes with green chiles
1/3 cup shredded Daiya vegan cheddar
1/3 cup shredded Daiya vegan pepperjack
1/3 cup shredded Daiya vegan mozzarella
2 tablespoons chopped cilantro

1   Preheat the oven to 375°F. Grease a 7 by 11-inch baking dish and line the bottom with half of the tortilla chips. Use the palm of your hand to press down on the chips and crush them a bit.

2   Heat 1 tablespoon of the olive oil in a large heavy pan over medium heat. Add the onion and cook for 2 minutes, stirring often, until slightly softened. Add the garlic and cook, stirring, for 1 minute more. Add the chili powder, cumin, and turkey meat, increase the heat to medium-high, and cook for 5 minutes, breaking up the turkey into crumbles with a spatula or wooden spoon. Cook until it's no longer pink. Season with salt and freshly ground pepper. Spoon over the tortilla chips in the baking dish.

3   Heat the remaining 1 tablespoon olive oil in the pan over medium heat. Add the beans and use a potato masher or the back of a fork to smash the beans. Heat through, about 2 minutes. Stir in the lime juice. Spoon the beans over the turkey layer in the baking dish. Top the bean layer with the diced tomatoes and a pinch of salt. Top the tomato layer with the remaining tortilla chips. Press down on the chips with the palm of your hand to crush them a bit.

4   Combine the three cheeses and sprinkle over the top of the casserole. Bake for 15 minutes in the center of the oven. Then put the pan under the broiler, 6 inches from the heat source, and cook for 2 to 3 minutes more, until the cheese has really melted and is just starting to brown.

5   Cut into 6 servings. Top with a sprinkling of cilantro.

Chicken Noodle Casserole

About as classic as apple pie, this all-American dish always reminds me of playing board games at my neighbors' house as a kid. Their last name was "Games"—no joke. Their mom often made tuna noodle casserole. My mother didn't, so it holds a special place in my heart as something exotic. The trick to making this allergy-friendly was to find a replacement for Campbell's cream of mushroom soup, which is the traditional base. I came up with my own recipe for cream of mushroom soup, then to make the rest of the recipe allergy-friendly I subbed rice milk for cow's milk and used vegan cheese, chicken instead of tuna, and gluten-free flour and pasta. The result? Tastes just like the original.

Use your food processor to chop the mushrooms in less than 30 seconds. Now that's easy cooking!

SERVES 4 TO 6

8	ounces gluten-free spiral or fusilli pasta
3	slices allergy-friendly white bread
1	tablespoon Earth Balance soy-free buttery spread
2	tablespoons olive oil
½	cup chopped yellow onion
10	ounces sliced white mushrooms, coarsely chopped
½	teaspoon dried thyme
	Pinch of ground nutmeg
2	tablespoons superfine brown rice flour
1	cup rice milk, warm
1½	cups chicken broth, warm
½	teaspoon salt
	Freshly ground pepper
½	cup shredded Daiya vegan mozzarella
10 to 12	ounces canned cooked chicken or turkey, well drained and flaked
1	cup frozen peas

1 Preheat the oven to 475°F.

2 Bring a large pot of water to a boil over high heat. Cook the pasta according to the package instructions, until al dente, about 10 minutes. Drain.

3 Meanwhile, tear the bread into quarters and pulse in a food processor until you have coarse crumbs.

4 Melt the buttery spread in a large heavy pan or Dutch oven over medium-high heat. Add the breadcrumbs and cook, stirring, until toasted, about 3 minutes. Transfer to a bowl and set aside. Wipe out the pan.

5 Heat the olive oil over medium heat. Add the onion and mushrooms and cook, stirring often, for 4 minutes, until slightly softened. Add the thyme and nutmeg and cook, stirring, for 2 minutes more, until aromatic.

6   Sprinkle the mushrooms with the brown rice flour and cook, stirring, until aromatic, 2 minutes. Add the rice milk and chicken broth to the pan, then the salt and a few turns of pepper. Increase the heat to medium-high and cook for 4 minutes, stirring with a wooden spoon. Puree with a handheld immersion blender, or use a regular blender and return the puree to the pot. If you're pureeing with a handheld blender, you may need to tip the pot slightly to submerge the blender (use a pot holder or an oven mitt).

7   Add the vegan mozzarella to the mushroom puree. Stir in the pasta. Add the chicken and peas, and stir gently. Transfer to a lightly greased shallow 2-quart baking dish. Sprinkle with the breadcrumbs. Bake for 8 to 10 minutes, until golden and beginning to bubble up around the sides.

Chicken and Sausage Paella

Paella is not usually a quick cooking dish, taking upward of an hour and a quarter—particularly if you make it with Arborio rice, which takes its time. Not so anymore. With the change to long grain basmati rice, and your trusty pal the microwave, you can now make paella in 30 minutes or less. Additionally, paella is often made with super allergenic ingredients, such as clam or fish broth and shellfish. I use a low-sodium chicken broth instead, and a highly flavorful chorizo or andouille sausage ensures you won't miss those clams and shrimp one tiny bit.

Buy prechopped onions or use your handy-dandy Vidalia Chop Wizard (see page 23) to speed your prep with the onion and bell pepper. Dicing veggies was never so easy. (And no, though I understand why you might think so, I am not a spokesperson for the Vidalia Chop Wizard.)

SERVES 6

- 1 cup long grain basmati rice
- 2¹⁄₂ cups low-sodium chicken broth
- 1 pound chicken tenders, cut crosswise into 1-inch pieces
- ³⁄₈ teaspoon smoked Spanish paprika
  Salt and freshly ground pepper
- 3 tablespoons olive oil
- 1 cup chopped yellow onion
- 8 ounces chorizo, andouille, linguica, or kielbasa, cut into ¹⁄₄-inch-thick rounds
- 1 red bell pepper, diced
- 3 cloves garlic, minced or pressed
- ¹⁄₄ teaspoon saffron, crushed
- ¹⁄₂ teaspoon dried oregano
- 1 (14.5-ounce) can diced tomatoes
- ³⁄₄ cup frozen peas
- 1 tablespoon chopped fresh parsley, plus more for garnish

1 Combine the rice with 1¹⁄₂ cups of the chicken broth in a microwave-safe container. Cover and microwave for 10 minutes.

2 Meanwhile, sprinkle the chicken tenders with the paprika and some salt and pepper. Heat 2 tablespoons of the olive oil in a large heavy pan or Dutch oven over medium-high heat until starting to shimmer. Add the chicken and cook for 2 minutes per side, until lightly browned. Transfer to a plate and set aside.

3 Add the remaining 1 tablespoon olive oil to the pan. Add the onion and sausage and cook for 5 minutes, stirring often. Add the bell pepper, garlic, saffron, oregano, and ¹⁄₄ teaspoon of salt and cook, stirring, for 2 minutes more. Add the remaining 1 cup chicken broth, bring to a boil, and deglaze the pan by scraping up any browned bits along the bottom, 1 minute or so. Stir in the tomatoes, partly cooked rice, and chicken, bring to a simmer, reduce the heat to medium, and cook, loosely covered, for 8 minutes more or until the liquid is absorbed. Add the peas and heat through for 2 minutes. Add salt and pepper to taste, toss with the parsley, and serve hot, sprinkled with a little more parsley.

Chicken Potpie with Biscuits

Chicken potpie is one of my son Lennon's all-time favorites. He's a casserole kind of kid. But rolling out a crust and baking up a pie isn't possible in 30 minutes or less. Plus, I secretly prefer potpie made with biscuits. I like the filling poured over the biscuits, and eating it with a knife and fork, while Lennon makes his into a potpie sandwich, using the biscuit like a bun.

This biscuit recipe has been refined from The Allergen-Free Baker's Handbook. *Leftover rotisserie chicken works great here.*

SERVES 4

BISCUITS

- 2 cups Authentic Foods GF Classical Blend flour or Basic Gluten-Free Flour Mix (page 48)
- ½ teaspoon xanthan gum
- 1 tablespoon baking powder
- ½ teaspoon salt
- ½ cup dairy-free, soy-free vegetable shortening, chilled
- 1 cup plain vegan yogurt

FILLING

- 2 tablespoons olive oil
- 1 stalk celery, chopped
- ½ cup frozen pearl onions, defrosted (1 minute in the microwave does it)
- 2 tablespoons superfine brown rice flour
- ¼ teaspoon dried thyme
  Pinch of cayenne pepper
- 1 cup chicken broth
- ¼ cup rice milk
  Salt
- ¾ cup frozen peas and carrots
- 2 cups diced cooked chicken
- 2 teaspoons freshly squeezed lemon juice
  Freshly ground pepper
- 2 tablespoons chopped parsley

1   Preheat the oven to 475°F. Line a baking sheet with parchment paper.

2   To make the biscuits, in a large bowl, whisk together the flour mix, xanthan gum, baking powder, and salt. Cut in the chilled shortening, using a pastry blender, two knives, or your fingers, until you have pea-size crumbs. Add the yogurt and stir until just combined, making sure you incorporate the crumbs at the bottom of the bowl.

3   Flour a work surface lightly with a little gluten-free flour mix and turn out the dough. Gently pat the dough into a ¾-inch-thick disk, pressing in any loose bits. Don't overhandle the dough.

4   Use a 2½-inch floured biscuit cutter to cut out the biscuits. Cut them as close together as possible. Gather together the scraps and reshape into a disk to cut out the last couple of biscuits; you will have 8 total. Transfer the biscuits to the baking sheet. Bake in the center of the oven for 20 minutes, until golden.

5   Meanwhile, make the filling. Heat the olive oil in a heavy pot over medium heat. Add the celery and pearl onions and cook, stirring a few times, for 2 minutes or until slightly softened. Add the brown rice flour to the celery and onions and sprinkle in the thyme and cayenne and cook, stirring, for 2 minutes, until golden and aromatic. Combine the broth and rice milk in a glass measuring cup and heat for 1 minute in the microwave.

6   Add the warmed broth–rice milk mixture to the celery and onion mixture a little at a time, stirring vigorously. Add a pinch of salt and cook at a simmer for about 2 minutes, until thickened. Add the peas and carrots, chicken, and lemon juice. Heat through at a simmer, 2 minutes more. Adjust the salt and pepper to taste. Serve over split biscuits with a sprinkling of chopped parsley.

CHICKEN
and
TURKEY

Chicken and turkey are probably the most kid-friendly proteins on the menu. And chicken is pretty much a staple for anyone going allergy-free. I know I practically lived on grilled chicken and rice when I was first put on a diet avoiding the top eight allergens. But grilled chicken breast can get awfully boring day in and day out. There is so much more to chicken! Nuggets, tenders, and cutlets are all favorites on my table. And yes, they can be made allergy-free, in an endless variety of ways.

Chicken and turkey are not only extremely versatile, but they also share the time-saver benefits of being quick cooking (when boneless) and of being relatively inexpensive, high-quality proteins. We often eat chicken in one form or another several nights a week.

In this chapter, you'll find an array of recipes, from Italian-American staples such as chicken Parmesan and saltimbocca to good old-fashioned comfort foods like mini turkey meatloaves, oven-fried chicken, chicken tenders, and chicken à la king. I've also included Asian-inspired dishes like chicken lettuce cups, Thai turkey larb, and teriyaki chicken thighs. There is something in here for every night of the week, with enough variety to prevent your family from muttering, "Chicken again?" Instead, they will be clamoring, "Chicken again!"—a demand you can easily meet.

Oven-Fried Chicken with Carrot Apple Slaw

Fried chicken used to be a once a year indulgence. Not anymore! With this low-fat oven-fried version, I can make fried chicken once a week. It's succulent and crunchy, and the tangy carrot apple slaw is a perfect light complement. Fried chicken and coleslaw just got healthy!

To crush the cornflakes, put them in a plastic bag and roll them with a rolling pin—or you can just crush them with your hands. Express-lane the slaw by buying shredded purple cabbage and shredded carrots.

SERVES 4

OVEN-FRIED CHICKEN

- 1/3 cup Earth Balance soy-free buttery spread, melted
- 1 tablespoon Dijon mustard
- 1/4 teaspoon garlic powder
- 1/4 teaspoon salt
- 1/4 teaspoon pepper
- 1/2 teaspoon hot sauce, such as Tabasco
- 1 1/4 pounds chicken cutlets
- 1 1/4 cups crushed cornflakes
- 1/4 teaspoon plus a big pinch of poultry seasoning
- 1/4 teaspoon plus a big pinch of sweet paprika
  Big pinch of cayenne pepper
- 1/2 cup plus 2 tablespoons shredded Daiya vegan mozzarella

CARROT APPLE SLAW

- 3 cups shredded purple cabbage
- 1/2 cup shredded carrot
- 2 Fuji apples, peeled, cored, and shredded
- 1/4 cup raisins
- 2 teaspoons rice milk
- 2 tablespoons rice vinegar
- 2 tablespoons orange juice
- 1 teaspoon agave nectar
- 4 tablespoons olive oil
  Salt

1   To make the chicken, preheat the oven to 400°F. Line a baking tray with aluminum foil. Spray the foil with cooking spray or grease lightly with olive or canola oil.

2   In a wide shallow dish, combine the melted buttery spread with the mustard, garlic powder, salt, pepper, and hot sauce.

3   Rinse and pat dry the cutlets. If they are not already ¼ inch thick, place them between two sheets of waxed paper and pound thin.

4   In another wide shallow dish, combine the cornflake crumbs with the poultry seasoning, paprika, and cayenne and toss. Toss in the vegan mozzarella.

5   Dip the cutlets in the buttery spread mixture, then dredge them in the cornflake mixture, using your fingers to press the coating onto the cutlets so it adheres. Transfer to the prepared baking tray.

6   Bake the cutlets for 25 minutes, until cooked through.

7   Meanwhile, make the slaw by tossing together the cabbage, carrot, apples, and raisins in a bowl. In a small bowl, whisk together the rice milk, rice vinegar, orange juice, and agave nectar. Whisk in the olive oil 1 tablespoon at a time. Pour the dressing over the slaw, toss well, sprinkle with a little salt, and toss again. Cover and refrigerate until ready to serve.

Chicken Tenders

This go-to recipe is always a favorite with kids. I return to this one over and over again. The trick to this recipe is an olive oil and rice milk emulsion that stands in for the egg traditionally used in breading the tenders; it creates a lovely golden, crispy tender. If you have leftovers, reheat them in the oven at 375°F for 10 to 15 minutes.

SERVES 4

1   pound chicken tenders
¾   cup coconut milk (shake can well
      before measuring)
½   cup cornstarch or tapioca starch,
      plus more as needed
2   tablespoons rice milk
4   tablespoons olive oil
1   cup gluten-free breadcrumbs (I use Ener-G)
      Salt and freshly ground pepper
3   cups canola oil
½   lemon
      Sea salt for serving
      Ketchup for serving

1   In a bowl, combine the chicken with the coconut milk.

2   Spread the cornstarch on a plate or wide shallow dish. Pour the rice milk into a second wide shallow dish. Add the olive oil to the rice milk 1 tablespoon at a time, whisking well after each addition, until creamy and beginning to thicken. Spread the breadcrumbs on a wide shallow dish. Season with salt and pepper and toss well.

3   Working quickly, remove a chicken tender from the coconut milk, roll it in the cornstarch, turn it in the rice milk mixture, then coat with the breadcrumbs. Set on a clean plate or platter. Repeat with the remaining tenders. You may have to wash your hands a couple of times during this process if the starch clumps up on them. Dip using your left hand for wet ingredients, right for dry.

4   Heat the canola oil in a medium-size deep sauté pan or Dutch oven over medium-high heat until really hot, but not smoking. It should be rippling. Drop a tiny piece of breading in to see if it sizzles— that means it's ready.

5   Cook the tenders in two batches, being sure not to overcrowd the pan, until they are deeply golden, about 3 minutes per side, or 6 minutes total. Remove from the pan with tongs, letting extra oil drip off, and place on a serving platter lined with paper towels. Squeeze with a little lemon juice and sprinkle with a little sea salt. Serve hot, with ketchup.

Quick Coq au Vin and Asparagus with Hollandaise Sauce

Quick coq au vin sounds like an oxymoron, like "jumbo shrimp." How can it be quick when it's coq au vin, the famously slow-braised dish beloved by Julia Child? Given my love of this hearty, flavorful meal, I decided that where there's a will, there's a way. I would make it in 30 minutes, and I would make it allergy-free. I can almost hear Julia saying, "What? No butter?!" But I'm pretty sure even she'd agree you really don't miss it. This version is delicious, allergy-friendly, quick, and easy. Serve with rice, noodles with a little Earth Balance soy-free buttery spread, or potatoes. For a little extra French flavor, serve with the Asparagus with Hollandaise Sauce.

SERVES 4

4   boneless, skinless chicken thighs
    (about 1¼ pounds total)
    Salt
    Freshly ground pepper
2   tablespoons olive oil
2   slices thick-cut bacon, diced
10 ounces sliced white or cremini mushrooms
1   cup frozen pearl onions, thawed and
    patted dry
3   carrots, chopped
1   teaspoon dried thyme
2   tablespoons superfine brown rice flour
1   cup dry red wine
1   cup chicken broth
1   tablespoon tomato paste
    Chopped fresh parsley

1   Rinse the chicken, pat dry, and trim off any fat. Halve the thighs for a total of 8 pieces. Season well with salt and pepper.

2   Heat the olive oil in a large casserole over medium-high heat until really hot and starting to shimmer. Add the chicken and cook for 4 minutes, until golden brown, then flip using a spatula or tongs. Add the bacon, sprinkling it around the chicken. Cook the chicken for 4 minutes more, until golden on both sides. Transfer the chicken to a plate and set aside.

3   Add the mushrooms, onions, carrots, and thyme. Cook for 4 minutes, stirring occasionally, until the mushrooms are tender. Sprinkle with the brown rice flour and cook, stirring often, for 2 minutes. Increase the heat to high, add the wine, and deglaze the pan by scraping up any browned bits on the bottom, about 1 minute. Add the chicken broth, tomato paste, and ¼ teaspoon salt. Reduce the heat to medium and simmer rapidly for 6 minutes, stirring often.

4   Return the chicken to the pan, spooning the sauce over the top. Cook for 8 minutes more, until the chicken is cooked through, turning it once halfway through.

5   Serve hot, sprinkled with a little parsley.

. . . continued

ASPARAGUS WITH HOLLANDAISE SAUCE

Hollandaise is traditionally made with eggs, one of the top eight food allergens. To replace eggs, vegan versions of the classic sauce usually rely on silken tofu. However, silken tofu (which is made from soy) is also among the top eight food allergens. So I had to put on my thinking cap to adapt this recipe.

I replaced the eggs and/or silken tofu with a rice milk and olive and canola oil emulsion, and added a smidgen of turmeric and a little nutritional yeast for the lovely buttercup hue and also a flavor boost. And, of course, I used lemon juice, because that zip of acidity is the backbone of all hollandaise sauces. As a bonus, this hollandaise is vegan, too, so there's no salmonella risk.

Remember when you make this that slow and steady wins the race. Add the oil a little at a time to achieve the creamiest result.

- ½ cup rice milk, cold
- 4 teaspoons freshly squeezed lemon juice, plus more if needed
- 1 tablespoon nutritional yeast
- ⅛ teaspoon cayenne pepper
- ⅛ teaspoon turmeric
- 1 small clove garlic, minced or pressed
- ¼ teaspoon xanthan gum
- 6 tablespoons olive oil
- 6 tablespoons canola oil
- ½ teaspoon fine sea salt
- 1 bunch asparagus (about 1½ pounds)

1   To make the hollandaise, combine the rice milk with the lemon juice, nutritional yeast, cayenne, and turmeric in a blender. Blend on high speed until the spices disperse. Add the garlic and the xanthan gum and mix on high speed until foamy.

2   With the blender running on high speed, use a liquid measuring cup to pour the oils, a little at a time, through the hole in the lid of the blender, until the hollandaise begins to emulsify.

3   Add the salt, taste, and adjust the salt and lemon juice to taste if desired. You'll have about 1½ cups.

4   To make the asparagus, trim or break off the tough ends. Set up a steamer basket in a pot, fill the bottom of the pot with water, and bring to a boil over medium-high heat. Add the asparagus to the steamer basket, cover, and steam until the asparagus is bright green and tender but still somewhat crisp, 3 to 6 minutes. Thinner asparagus will cook more quickly, so keep an eye on it. Remove the asparagus from the steamer.

5   Serve with the hollandaise drizzled over the top. Transfer the remaining hollandaise to a jar and store, tightly covered, in the refrigerator for up to 1 week. Bring to room temperature before serving.

Chicken à la King

This retro dish is so kid-friendly, I actually watched my son's best friend Domenic lick the plate after I served it to him. Though it has a fancy royal-sounding name, it hails from a hotel in Brighton Beach, New York. It's just good humble food, fit for kings and your kids, too. The trick to making this dish allergy-friendly was in replacing the traditional dairy (cream), eggs, and wheat flour. Serve this over rice or toasted allergy-friendly white bread buttered with a little Earth Balance soy-free buttery spread. Use your Vidalia Chop Wizard (see page 23) with the small grid to mince the bell pepper in less than 30 seconds, and use the larger grid to dice your onions.

SERVES 4 TO 6

- 3/4 cup rice milk
- 2 tablespoons freshly squeezed lemon juice
- 1 teaspoon salt
- 1 1/2 pounds boneless, skinless chicken breast, cut into 1-inch cubes
- 2 tablespoons olive oil
- 1 cup diced yellow onion
- 8 ounces sliced white mushrooms
- 1 red bell pepper, finely minced
- 1/4 teaspoon freshly ground pepper
- 2 tablespoons superfine brown rice flour
- 1/2 cup sweet Marsala
- 3/4 cup chicken broth
- 2 tablespoons chopped fresh parsley

1   Combine the rice milk, lemon juice, and salt in a large bowl. Add the chicken pieces, toss to coat, and set aside.

2   Heat the olive oil over medium-high heat in a large sauté pan or Dutch oven, until just starting to ripple. Add the onion and cook, stirring occasionally, until tender, 2 to 3 minutes. Add the mushrooms, bell pepper, and black pepper and cook, stirring occasionally, until softened, 5 minutes.

3   Sprinkle the brown rice flour over the vegetables and cook, stirring, for 2 minutes, until aromatic. Add the Marsala and deglaze the pan, scraping up any browned bits on the bottom, about 1 minute. Add the chicken broth, bring to a simmer, reduce the heat to medium, and cook for about 3 minutes, until starting to thicken up to the consistency of a rich gravy. Pour in the chicken soaking liquid (the rice milk mixture) a little at a time, stirring as you go. Cook for a few minutes more, until it's starting to get creamy. Add the chicken, reduce the heat to medium-low, and cook for 10 minutes, until the chicken is cooked through. Sprinkle with the parsley.

Chicken "Parmesan" with Simple Red Sauce

Ah, chicken parm, the most ubiquitous of Italian-American favorites. Who doesn't love this dish? Even when it's soggy and poorly executed, as it so often is, it's still delicious. But it's also usually an allergen bomb, between the eggs, the wheat breadcrumbs for breading, and the mounds of cheese and butter. Enter allergy-friendly chicken parm. Yup, that's right. Beloved even by my husband, who grew up in the Bronx near Arthur Avenue (the real Little Italy of New York City), and then on Long Island in the same town as that Italian restaurant Billy Joel is always singing about (you know, "bottle of red, bottle of white . . ."). This is definitely a dish for all ages, so whether you eat it accompanied by a glass of Chianti or a cup of apple juice, buon appetito!

.... **SERVES 4**

SIMPLE RED SAUCE
- 1 (28-ounce) can crushed tomatoes
- 1 tablespoon olive oil
- 2 cloves garlic, finely minced or pressed
- 2 tablespoons chopped fresh basil
- ¼ cup shredded Daiya vegan mozzarella

- ¼ cup cornstarch or tapioca starch
- ¾ cup gluten-free breadcrumbs (I prefer Ener-G) Salt and freshly ground pepper
- ½ teaspoon dried oregano
- 2 tablespoons rice milk
- 6 tablespoons olive oil
- 4 (4-ounce) chicken cutlets, ¼ inch thick (see page 82, step 1)
- ½ cup shredded Daiya vegan mozzarella Fresh basil for garnish

....

1 Preheat the oven to 450°F.

2 To make the sauce, combine all the ingredients for the sauce in a heavy pan over medium heat. Bring to a simmer and cook for 5 minutes, stirring often. Set aside.

3 Pour the cornstarch into a shallow bowl and set aside. Combine the breadcrumbs with some salt and pepper and the oregano in another shallow bowl; set aside. Pour the rice milk into a third shallow bowl. Whisk in 4 tablespoons of the olive oil, 1 tablespoon at a time, until you have a creamy emulsion.

4 Turn one chicken cutlet in the cornstarch, coating both sides. Lift out, shaking off the extra cornstarch, and dip in the rice milk mixture, then turn in the breadcrumbs to coat. Set aside. Repeat with the remaining 3 cutlets.

5 Heat 1 tablespoon of the olive oil in a large heavy pan over medium-high heat until just starting to ripple. Add the cutlets and cook for 2 minutes, then add the remaining 1 tablespoon olive oil, turn the chicken, and cook for 2 minutes more. Transfer to a nonstick baking pan. Spray the tops of the cutlets with a little cooking spray and bake for 5 minutes.

6 Meanwhile, rewarm the sauce over medium heat. Remove the baking pan from the oven, flip the chicken, and top each cutlet with 2 tablespoons of the sauce. Sprinkle the vegan mozzarella evenly over the cutlets, and return to the oven to bake for 8 more minutes, until the cheese has melted and is bubbling. Serve garnished with a few basil leaves.

Chicken Piccata

Chicken piccata is a tangy and light way to cook up chicken cutlets, and it pairs well with plain linguine or spaghetti. While I do love veal piccata too, after looking into the whole concept of "free-range" veal, I decided to take it off my menu (after all, veal, by nature, doesn't range anywhere—it stays put, to keep it tender). So I'm stickin' with chicken. (Plus, chicken is cheaper!) Serve this with plain linguine, tossed with a little olive oil and salt.

SERVES 4 TO 6

1½ **pounds chicken cutlets**
¼ **cup superfine brown rice flour**
   Salt and freshly ground pepper
2 **tablespoons olive oil**
¼ **cup freshly squeezed lemon juice**
½ **cup chicken broth**
2 **tablespoons capers (nonpareils), drained**
1 **tablespoon Earth Balance soy-free buttery spread**
2 **tablespoons chopped fresh parsley**

1   Place the chicken cutlets between two sheets of waxed paper and pound until ¼ inch thick. You really want to make sure they are this thin, for optimum tenderness.

2   Put the brown rice flour in a shallow bowl. Sprinkle the cutlets on both sides with salt and pepper, dredge them in the rice flour to coat well, and set aside.

3   Heat a large sauté pan over medium-high heat. Add the olive oil and heat until it starts to ripple. Add the cutlets, being sure not to overcrowd them. Cook for about 3 minutes per side, until they are a lovely golden brown. Remove from the pan to a plate, and cover to keep warm.

4   Add the lemon juice, chicken broth, and capers to the pan and bring to a boil, stirring to deglaze and scraping up all the lovely browned bits from the bottom of the pan. Simmer the sauce for 4 minutes, stirring often, to reduce by at least half. Remove from the heat, add the buttery spread, and swirl until it's completely dissolved. Put the cutlets on plates, spoon the sauce over each, and sprinkle with the parsley.

Chicken Saltimbocca

I love the derivation of the name of this dish. Saltimbocca means "jump in the mouth," which is exactly what you'll want this chicken to do! This is fabulous with quick polenta (see page 95), Roasted Fingerling Potatoes (page 104), or sautéed broccoli.

SERVES 6

- 3 large boneless, skinless chicken breasts (1½ pounds total)
- 12 fresh sage leaves
- 6 slices prosciutto (3 to 4 ounces total)
- ¼ cup superfine brown rice flour
  Salt and freshly ground pepper
- 2 tablespoons olive oil
- ½ cup white wine
- 1 cup chicken broth

1   If the chicken breasts still have their tenders attached, remove them and set them aside (you can use them in another recipe tomorrow night). Slice the breasts into halves vertically, for a total of 6 pieces. Place each piece between two sheets of waxed paper and pound them to about ¼ inch thick. Place a sage leaf on top of each piece of chicken. Set the 6 remaining sage leaves aside for later. Wrap each breast in a slice of prosciutto, pressing it down to stick to the chicken, covering the sage leaves.

2   Put the brown rice flour in a shallow bowl and season with salt and pepper. Dredge the chicken breasts in the flour, shaking off any extra.

3   Heat the olive oil in a large (12-inch) heavy pan over medium-high heat until just starting to ripple. Cook the chicken pieces sage side down first, for 4 to 5 minutes, then flip and cook for 4 to 5 minutes more, until golden brown.

4   Transfer the chicken to a platter and tent loosely with aluminum foil. Decrease the heat to medium; add the wine to the pan, bring to a simmer, and deglaze, scraping up any brown bits, about 1 minute. Add the broth, increase the heat to medium-high, and cook at a rapid simmer, stirring often, for 8 minutes, until thickened up to a rich gravy (it will be reduced by about half). Return the chicken to the pan. Warm for about 2 minutes and serve with the sauce, garnished with the 6 remaining sage leaves.

Roasted Chicken with Rosemary, Kalamata Olives, and Lemon

This is a great one to throw together when you have unexpected company. It seems fancy, but it's as easy as can be to prepare. One of your best friends in this dish is a mini chopper. Use it to mince your garlic and your rosemary. And look for jarred split kalamata olives to save yourself that prep time, too.

SERVES 6

3 large bone-in, skin-on split chicken breasts (2½ to 2¾ pounds total), cut in half crosswise (get the butcher to do it for you, or use a cleaver)
Salt and freshly ground pepper

2 tablespoons olive oil

1 tablespoon minced garlic

1 tablespoon minced fresh rosemary

1 lemon, cut into 8 wedges

15 kalamata olives, split and pitted, or 30 olive halves

2 tablespoons white wine
White rice for serving (optional)

1   Preheat the oven to 450°F.

2   Rinse the chicken, then pat it dry. Season with salt and pepper.

3   Heat the olive oil in a large heavy casserole or Dutch oven over medium-high heat until the oil is starting to shimmer, about 2 minutes. Cook the chicken, skin side down, for 5 to 6 minutes, until crispy and browned. Flip, being careful to keep the skin attached to the breast, and cook for 5 minutes more.

4   Remove the pan from the heat. Sprinkle with the garlic and rosemary. Add the lemon wedges and olives and drizzle in the white wine. Bake in the center of the oven for 18 minutes, until cooked through. Serve with the white rice, spooning the sauce over both the rice and the chicken.

Chicken Lettuce Cups with Hoisin Sauce

This dish taught me once and for all about the brilliance of a food processor. If you just pulse your veggies, they're diced small in literally seconds. And you can mince your garlic and ginger in about the same time. Seriously, use that food processor with the blade setting to get finely chopped carrots, celery, red bell pepper, and water chestnuts with almost no effort at all. You can even use it to chop up the green onions, though it's more of a shred than a chop.

Allergy-friendly hoisin sauce is a new concept, because the traditional version is dependent on soy and wheat/gluten. This fresh, sweet, and savory version will have you dipping all your favorite Chinese foods in sauce again, only now it'll have a lot less sodium and lots more safe-for-you hoisin flavor.

SERVES 4

- 1 tablespoon canola oil
- 2 cloves garlic, finely minced or pressed
- 1 teaspoon minced ginger
- ½ cup small-dice carrot
- ½ cup small-dice celery heart
- ½ cup small-dice red bell pepper
- 3 green onions, white and green parts, chopped
- 1 (5-ounce) can water chestnuts, chopped to pea size
- 1½ pounds ground dark meat chicken
- 2 tablespoons chicken broth
- Salt
- 6 tablespoons Hoisin Sauce (recipe follows)
- 1 tablespoon rice vinegar
- Freshly ground pepper
- Butter or iceberg lettuce leaves
- Sriracha sauce (optional)

1 Heat the canola oil in a nonstick wok or skillet over medium heat. Add the garlic and ginger and cook, stirring, for 30 seconds, until fragrant and golden.

2 Add the carrot, celery, bell pepper, green onions, and water chestnuts and cook for 4 minutes, stirring often.

3 Add the ground chicken and broth and increase the heat to high. Sprinkle with a large pinch of salt. Cook, stirring often with a wooden spoon or spatula and breaking up the chicken into crumbles, for 4 minutes, until no longer pink and starting to brown.

4 Add 3 tablespoons of the Hoisin Sauce, reserving the rest for serving alongside the lettuce cups. Stir in the rice vinegar, bring to a simmer, reduce the heat to low, and cook at a slow simmer for 3 minutes. Adjust the salt and pepper to taste.

5 Serve with the lettuce leaves. Each diner makes his or her own bundles by spooning about 2 tablespoons of chicken into each leaf, toping with a little of the remaining 3 tablespoons Hoisin Sauce, wrapping it up, and eating! (I like to add a little Sriracha sauce to mine, too.)

. . . continued

HOISIN SAUCE

- ¼ cup coconut amino acids
- ⅔ cup orange juice
- 2 cloves garlic, finely minced or pressed
- 1 teaspoon minced ginger
- ⅛ teaspoon cayenne pepper
- ¼ teaspoon Chinese five-spice powder
- ¼ teaspoon salt
- ¼ cup brown sugar
- 1 tablespoon molasses
- 2 teaspoons cider vinegar
- ¼ cup cold water
- 1 tablespoon cornstarch or tapioca starch

Combine the coconut amino acids, orange juice, garlic, ginger, cayenne, five-spice powder, and salt in a small heavy pot and stir well. Bring to a simmer over medium heat. Add the sugar and molasses and stir well. Add the vinegar. In a small bowl, whisk together the cold water with the cornstarch until smooth, then add it to the pot. Bring to a simmer. Reduce the heat to low and cook, stirring with a wooden spoon, until thickened up a bit, about 4 minutes. Makes 1¼ cups that will keep for 1 to 2 weeks, covered, in the refrigerator.

Teriyaki Chicken Thighs

These teriyaki chicken thighs—low in fat, high in protein, succulent, and flavorful—have become a go-to favorite at my house, particularly on Tuesdays when the kids and I don't get home from break-dancing class until eight o'clock. Use your garlic press, and your mini chopper to mince the ginger, for a super speedy prep.

SERVES 4

TERIYAKI SAUCE
- 6 tablespoons coconut amino acids
- 3 cloves garlic, finely minced or pressed
- 1½ teaspoons finely minced ginger
- ⅛ teaspoon cayenne pepper
- ¾ teaspoon salt
- ⅜ teaspoon freshly ground pepper
- 3 tablespoons brown sugar
- 1½ tablespoons honey
- 3 tablespoons rice vinegar
- 3 tablespoons dry sherry

- 3 pounds bone-in chicken thighs
- 1 tablespoon shelled hemp seeds (optional)
- 1 green onion, white and green parts, chopped

1   To make the sauce, combine all the sauce ingredients in a large bowl, stirring well to dissolve the brown sugar.

2   Preheat the broiler on high heat. Line the broiler pan with aluminum foil.

3   Remove the skin from the chicken. Rinse and pat the chicken dry, then add it to the sauce, turning to coat and spooning sauce over the top. Let rest for 5 minutes.

4   Transfer the chicken to the lined broiler pan, reserving the sauce. Cook the chicken thighs top-side down 4 inches from the heat source for 10 minutes or until crispy, rotating the pan halfway through. Flip the chicken and cook for 8 minutes more, rotating the pan after 4 minutes. Sprinkle the chicken with the hemp seeds and cook for 2 minutes more, until crispy.

5   Meanwhile, pour the sauce into a small saucepan and bring to a simmer over medium heat. Decrease the heat to medium-low and cook at a slow simmer for 16 to 20 minutes to reduce to a syrupy consistency.

6   To serve, drizzle the chicken with the sauce and garnish with the chopped green onion.

Mini Meatloaves with Quick and Easy Barbecue Sauce

Barbecue sauce is tricky for people with food allergies because it usually contains Worcestershire sauce, which has soy and anchovies in it. Additionally, so many commercial brands contain high-fructose corn syrup. So I derived this quick and easy allergy-free sauce, with which you'll soon be basting everything in sight. To start out, try it on these succulent, flavorful, perfect little meatloaves. To get $^3/_4$ cup of crushed cornflakes, pulse 2 cups of cornflakes in the food processor. Serve this with steamed green beans or Creamed Spinach (page 106).

SERVES 4

$1^1/_2$ teaspoons Ener-G egg replacer

5 tablespoons rice milk

$1^1/_2$ pounds ground dark meat turkey

$^1/_4$ cup minced fresh parsley

2 cloves garlic, finely minced or pressed

$^1/_2$ teaspoon salt

$^1/_4$ teaspoon pepper

7 tablespoons Quick and Easy Barbecue Sauce (recipe follows)

$^3/_4$ cup crushed cornflakes or gluten-free breadcrumbs

2 tablespoons canola oil

1   Preheat the oven to 425°F.

2   In a large bowl, whisk together the egg replacer and 2 tablespoons of the rice milk. Add the turkey, parsley, garlic, salt, pepper, 3 tablespoons of the barbecue sauce, and the remaining 3 tablespoons rice milk. Mix well. Add the cornflake crumbs, mixing well to combine. Mold into four 4 by 3-inch loaves, doming them slightly on the tops.

3   Heat the canola oil in a large oven-safe skillet over medium-high heat. Cook the loaves for 2 minutes, starting with the bottom (flatter) sides. Flip with a spatula and cook for 2 minutes more. Flip the meatloaves back so their domed sides are up. Spoon 1 tablespoon of the remaining barbecue sauce over each loaf. Transfer the skillet to the oven and bake for 20 minutes more, until cooked through and the top is deeply browned.

. . . continued

QUICK AND EASY BARBECUE SAUCE

¹/₂ cup ketchup

¹/₄ cup cider vinegar

3 tablespoons brown sugar

1 tablespoon molasses

1 tablespoon Dijon mustard

¹/₂ teaspoon powdered ginger

¹/₂ teaspoon garlic powder

1 teaspoon barbecue seasoning

¹/₄ teaspoon salt

¹/₄ teaspoon pepper

¹/₄ teaspoon chili powder

1 tablespoon canola oil

Combine all the ingredients in a small saucepan and bring to a boil over medium-high heat. Reduce the heat to low and simmer, loosely covered, for 5 minutes. Makes 1 cup that will keep for several weeks, covered, in the refrigerator.

Thai Turkey Larb

Larb is a traditional Thai dish that is very light and refreshing. It has almost no fat and is full of flavor. If you like it spicier, increase the chile sauce, or serve it with sliced Thai chiles. Use a food processor or mini chopper to mince the ginger and chop the red onion. I encourage you to make the fresh, preservative-free, spicy Asian chile sauce given here. It will knock your socks off. Use serrano, Thai, jalapeño, habanero, or Fresno chiles, or a combination of several. I make it with serrano or Thai chiles combined with habaneros, but I'm a hot sauce fanatic.

SERVES 4

1	stalk fresh lemongrass
1	teaspoon canola oil
1/2	cup finely chopped red onion
1	teaspoon minced ginger
1 1/2	pounds ground dark meat turkey
1/4	cup chicken broth
2	green onions, white and green parts, chopped
1/2	teaspoon salt
2	tablespoons chopped cilantro
2	tablespoons chopped fresh mint
1	teaspoon Sriracha or Thai Chile Sauce (recipe follows)
2	tablespoons freshly squeezed lime juice
1	tablespoon freshly squeezed lemon juice
1	tablespoon mirin
12	butter lettuce leaves
	Jasmine rice or sticky rice for serving (optional)

1   Cut the thick bottom of the lemongrass stalk into a 4-inch piece. Peel off the outer leaves if dry, then crush the piece with the flat side of your knife or a mallet, cut in half lengthwise, and finely chop crosswise.

2   Heat the canola oil in a large pan over medium-high heat. Add the onion, ginger, and lemongrass and cook for 2 minutes. Add the ground turkey and chicken broth and cook for 5 minutes, until the turkey is no longer pink.

3   Reduce the heat to medium, add the green onions and salt, and cook for 2 minutes. Stir in the cilantro and mint.

4   In a bowl, combine the chile sauce, lime juice, lemon juice, and mirin, stirring well. Add to the turkey, toss, and adjust the salt to taste.

5   Serve with lettuce leaves and rice, spooning the larb into the leaves and bundling up to eat.

. . . continued

Thai Turkey Larb, continued

THAI CHILE SAUCE

6 ounces fresh hot chiles
4 large cloves garlic
1 teaspoon fine sea salt
2 tablespoons sugar
2 tablespoons white vinegar

1 Stem the chiles and chop them into pieces. Combine with the garlic, salt, sugar, and vinegar in a mini chopper or food processor. Pulse until pureed.

2 Transfer to a small saucepan, bring to a simmer over medium heat, and cook for 5 minutes. Remove from the heat and set aside to cool. Transfer to a glass jar, cover tightly, and store in the fridge. Makes about 1/2 cup that will keep for several weeks, covered, in the refrigerator.

Turkey Cutlets with Polenta

Choice Batter is my new favorite allergy-free ingredient. It allows you to fry foods, while absorbing 50 percent less fat than traditional batter. Here I use it with thin turkey cutlets, which are a high protein alternative to chicken. Please note that the turkey cutlets need to be really thin, ¼ inch thick or less. You may also use thin chicken cutlets. You will need a candy or oil thermometer for this recipe, to make sure your oil is really hot— if it's not hot enough, the batter won't adhere properly.

SERVES 4

1   cup Choice Batter (see Resources)
¼   teaspoon cayenne pepper
½   teaspoon dried oregano
5   cups cold water
    Salt
    Canola oil for deep-frying
1   pound thin turkey cutlets
1   cup instant polenta
2   tablespoons Earth Balance soy-free
    buttery spread
    Simple Red Sauce (page 80), Quick Chunky
    Marinara (page 51), Hemp Seed Pesto
    (page 54), or, in a pinch, plain old ketchup

1   In a wide dish or bowl, combine the Choice Batter with the cayenne and oregano. Whisk well. Pour in 1 cup of the cold water and stir until smooth. Let rest for 5 minutes.

2   Put the remaining 4 cups water on to boil and sprinkle in some salt.

3   Pour canola oil at least 2 inches deep into a deep fryer, electric skillet, or deep frying pan and heat over high heat until it reaches 375°F on a candy or oil thermometer. When the oil is hot enough, drop in a tiny bit of batter to test. It should sizzle up fast.

4   While the oil heats, prepare the cutlets. Rinse the cutlets and pat them dry. Add the cutlets to the batter, turning to make sure they are well coated.

5   Cook the cutlets in two batches, being sure not to overcrowd the pan and giving them a quick swirl with the tongs right after you drop them into the oil. Cook until deeply golden, 2 minutes per side or 4 minutes total. Transfer to a paper towel–lined platter with tongs, letting extra oil drip into the pan as you lift the pieces out of it.

6   Add the polenta a little at a time to the boiling water and cook, stirring, for 3 minutes, until thick and creamy. Remove from the heat and stir in the buttery spread and a little salt to taste. Serve the cutlets alongside the polenta, with the sauce of your choice to taste, or just as is.

BEEF, PORK, *and* LAMB

Meat and I have a checkered past. When I was fifteen, I became a vegetarian. I stayed that way for the better part of thirteen years. Then one day, at a barbecue at my husband's (then-boyfriend's) parents' house, faced with a choice between steak, mushy macadamia-crusted orange roughy, or nothing, I uncharacteristically asked for the steak. And boy was it delicious! From there, it was like a switch was flipped, and I became obsessed with cooking meat. I was pan-frying chops and cooking up roasts, whole legs of lamb, and fresh hams in cider; I was buying game at the farmers' market in Union Square— venison, wild boar, rabbit, I kid you not—and nothing made me happier than a petite filet mignon. I must have been making up for years of anemia.

While I was pregnant with Lennon, the switch flipped back again, and I became disgusted by meat. In fact, I was disgusted by anything but bagels and ice cream. But once he was born, and diagnosed with multiple food allergies, I was put on a maternal avoidance diet while breastfeeding him, and then he too was on a strict allergy-free diet avoiding the top eight allergens. As he delved into the world of solid food, that love of meat came roaring back with a vengeance. My first cookbook, *The Whole Foods Allergy Cookbook*, was full of a lot of meat, because that's what I was eating while I wrote it. I found it difficult to get enough protein without eating meat, while avoiding dairy, eggs, soy, wheat, peanuts, tree nuts, fish, and shellfish. I got pretty friendly with the butcher. Then, for my next book, I wrote a vegan cookbook. But I digress. This is a meat chapter. And it's full of recipes that my meat-and-potatoes son Lennon loves.

Beef and Broccoli Stir-Fry

Cut your time in half on this recipe by shopping wisely—precut broccoli florets will simplify your life. Using beef tenderloin in this dish will ensure tenderness. If you'd rather use a more inexpensive cut of beef, then go for flank steak or tri tip, or use rib eye, and use a very sharp knife to cut across the grain into paper-thin slices. It will help tenderize the meat. Serve with white rice.

SERVES 4

1 pound beef tenderloin, fat trimmed

3 tablespoons Cybele's Soy-Free Soy Sauce (page 141) or coconut amino acids

3 tablespoons mirin

4 tablespoons canola oil

¼ cup chicken broth

1 tablespoon cornstarch or tapioca starch

2 teaspoons honey

¼ teaspoon freshly ground pepper

3 large cloves garlic, finely minced or pressed

1 tablespoon finely minced ginger

5 cups broccoli florets, blanched (see note)

Salt

1 Cut the beef into ¼-inch-thick slices. Cut the slices into rectangular pieces about ½ inch wide and 1 inch long. In a bowl, combine 1 tablespoon of the soy-free soy sauce with 1 tablespoon of the mirin and 1 tablespoon of the canola oil. Add the beef and toss well to coat with the marinade; set aside for 15 minutes.

2 In a small bowl, mix together the chicken broth, the remaining 2 tablespoons mirin, the remaining 2 tablespoons soy-free soy sauce, and the cornstarch, honey, and black pepper.

3 Place a wok over the highest possible heat. When it's hot, add 2 tablespoons of the canola oil to the center of the wok and swirl it around. Once it's just started hinting that it's about to smoke, add the beef. Stir-fry until it loses its raw color, 2 to 3 minutes. Remove from the wok and set aside; keep warm.

4 Add the remaining 1 tablespoon canola oil to the wok and swirl it around. Add the garlic and ginger and cook for about 5 seconds, then add the broccoli and stir-fry until heated through, 1 to 2 minutes. Stir the chicken broth mixture and add it to the wok. Return the beef to the wok. Sprinkle generously with salt, stir and toss well, and transfer to a warmed serving platter. Eat hot!

Note: To blanch broccoli, bring a pot of salted water to a boil, add the broccoli florets, and cook until tender but still crisp, 2 minutes. Drain and rinse with cold water.

Salisbury Steak with Mashed Potatoes

Give my kids gravy on anything and they'll smile. Which is why I worked particularly hard on this recipe. I did the gravy about seven different ways before I was satisfied it had the right color, thickness, and "yum" factor. If you or your loved ones are meat-and-potatoes types, then this is the meal for you. Add peas, and you've got an old-fashioned classic. The bonus? It's got a fraction of the sodium, no preservatives, no additives, and none of the allergens (wheat, soy, dairy, egg) I saw listed on the Salisbury steak dinners in the frozen foods aisle.

SERVES 4

MASHED POTATOES

- 2 pounds Yukon Gold potatoes, peeled and quartered
- 1/2 cup rice milk, warmed
- 4 tablespoons Earth Balance soy-free buttery spread
- 1/4 teaspoon salt

SALISBURY STEAK

- 2 tablespoons olive oil
- 1/2 large yellow onion, cut into two half-moons, then sliced thin vertically (3/4 cup)
- 1 clove garlic, pressed or minced
  Salt and freshly ground pepper
- 1/8 teaspoon smoked Spanish paprika
  Pinch of ground allspice
- 2 tablespoons plus 3/4 teaspoon superfine brown rice flour
- 1 3/4 cups plus 2 tablespoons beef broth
- 3 tablespoons ketchup
- 2 1/4 teaspoons freshly squeezed lemon juice
- 1 1/2 teaspoons honey
- 1 pound ground beef
- 6 tablespoons gluten-free breadcrumbs (I like Ener-G)
- 1 teaspoon Ener-G egg replacer mixed with 4 teaspoons water

1   To make the mashed potatoes, put the potatoes in a microwave-safe container, covered but with a slight opening. Cook for 10 minutes on high. Let rest, covered, for 5 minutes. Add the warm rice milk, buttery spread, and salt and use an electric hand mixer or potato masher to mash and mix.

2   Meanwhile, make the Salisbury steak. Heat 1 tablespoon of the olive oil in a large pan or casserole over medium heat. Add the onion, garlic, $1/4$ teaspoon of salt, $1/8$ teaspoon of pepper, paprika, and allspice. Cook, stirring often, for 3 minutes, until the onion has started to soften. Sprinkle with the brown rice flour and cook, stirring, for 2 minutes. Add the beef broth and simmer for a minute, deglazing and scraping up any browned bits on the bottom of the pan. Add the ketchup, lemon juice, and honey and stir to dissolve. Bring to a simmer, then remove from the heat and set aside.

3   Combine the ground beef with the breadcrumbs and egg replacer, using your hands to work it in well. Season with salt and pepper and mix. Divide the meat into four balls, then use the palms of your hands to flatten the balls into oval patties, 5 by 4 inches and $1/2$ inch thick.

4   Heat the remaining 1 tablespoon olive oil in a large skillet over medium-high heat. Once it is starting to ripple, add the patties. Cook for 3 minutes per side, flipping with a spatula, until deeply browned. Reduce the heat to low, pour the gravy over the patties, spooning it over the tops, and cook for 10 minutes, loosely covered, spooning sauce over the tops periodically. Serve with the mashed potatoes, spooning the gravy over both.

Beef Stroganoff with Buttery Noodles

I first ate stroganoff in Oslo, Norway, on a freezing December night. It was reindeer stroganoff. I felt pretty ambivalent about eating it, given our cultural love of Rudolf, but it was so darn tasty, I polished off seconds. Reindeer is hard to come by stateside, plus I doubt any of us could get our kids to eat it, so I've turned to a more conventional kind of meat. Good old top sirloin does the trick, with gusto. This one is super on a cold winter's night. Whether you're in Ohio or Oslo, it warms your soul and is fantastically comforting. Use Tinkyada pasta for this if you can find it: their fusilli is bigger, and more like traditional egg noodles.

SERVES 4

8 ounces gluten-free fusilli

3 tablespoons Earth Balance soy-free buttery spread

1 pound top sirloin steak, cut into 2 by $\frac{1}{2}$-inch pieces
   Kosher salt and freshly ground pepper

1 tablespoon olive oil

2 tablespoons finely minced yellow onion

6 ounces sliced mushrooms

2 tablespoons superfine brown rice flour

1 cup beef broth, warmed
   Pinch of ground nutmeg

$\frac{1}{4}$ cup plain vegan yogurt

1 teaspoon freshly squeezed lemon juice

1   Bring a large pot of water to a boil over high heat and cook the pasta according to the instructions on the package. Drain and toss with 2 tablespoons of the buttery spread.

2   Meanwhile, season the steak with salt and pepper. Heat the olive oil in a large skillet over medium-high heat, until really starting to shimmer. Add the steak and cook for 4 to 5 minutes, until browned on both sides. Transfer to a plate, and tent loosely with aluminum foil.

3   Melt the remaining 1 tablespoon of the buttery spread in a pan over medium heat. Add the minced onion and sliced mushrooms. Cook for 4 minutes, stirring often, until the mushrooms are starting to brown up. Sprinkle with the brown rice flour and cook, stirring, for 1 minute more. Add the broth, stirring constantly. Add a few turns of pepper and a pinch of nutmeg. Simmer, stirring, for 2 minutes, until thickened. Return the beef to the pan, turn to coat, stir in the yogurt and lemon juice, and heat through. Season with salt to taste and serve over the noodles.

Steak Salad

Strip steak and tenderloin are both incredibly tender, and perfect for steak salad. Wild baby arugula is wonderful with this if you can find it.

SERVES 4

- 1 small clove garlic, pressed or smashed in a mortar and pestle
- 1 teaspoon Dijon mustard
- 2 teaspoons brown sugar
- 1 tablespoon rice vinegar
- 1 tablespoon balsamic vinegar
- ¼ cup extra virgin olive oil
- 5 leaves fresh basil, coarsely chopped
- 2 cups baby arugula
- 2 cups chopped endive
- 2 cups chopped radicchio
  Salt and freshly ground pepper
- 2 (12-ounce) strip steaks or tenderloin steaks (1 inch thick)
- 1 tablespoon olive oil

1   In a small bowl, combine the garlic, mustard, and sugar. Add the rice vinegar and balsamic, and stir well. Whisk in the extra virgin olive oil 1 tablespoon at a time until the dressing has emulsified. Stir in the basil.

2   In a large bowl, toss together the arugula, endive, and radicchio. Toss with the dressing and season with salt and pepper. Divide the salad evenly among 4 plates.

3   Pat the steaks dry and season with salt and pepper. Heat a cast-iron skillet over medium-high heat and add the 1 tablespoon olive oil. Cook the steaks for 2 to 3 minutes per side, until browned and cooked to medium rare (cook longer if you like your steak more well done). Transfer the steak from the pan and slice thin. Divide the steak evenly among the 4 plates. Season to taste with salt and pepper.

Balsamic-Glazed Steak Tips with Roasted Fingerling Potatoes and Creamed Spinach

Although this dish might seem fancy, it's one of the easiest recipes in the book. My son Lennon is crazy for fingerling potatoes and loves swirling them in the balsamic glaze. Rosemary and balsamic really bring out the best in top sirloin, which pairs beautifully with the sweetness of the glaze. The Creamed Spinach is optional, but note that it is divine. It's rich and creamy, with absolutely no cream at all. I could eat the whole batch with a spoon.

SERVES 4

3 tablespoons Earth Balance soy-free buttery spread, at room temperature
2 teaspoons minced fresh rosemary
Kosher salt
1½ pounds top sirloin steak, cut into 2-inch chunks
Freshly ground pepper
1 tablespoon olive oil
2 tablespoons minced shallot
¼ cup balsamic vinegar
1 teaspoon honey
Roasted Fingerling Potatoes (recipe follows)
Creamed Spinach (recipe follows)

1 Combine the buttery spread with the minced rosemary and a big pinch of kosher salt. Mix well with a spoon until completely blended. Scoop out onto a piece of plastic wrap and roll into a cylinder. Chill in the freezer for 20 minutes.

2 Meanwhile, pat the steak tips dry and season with kosher salt and freshly ground pepper.

3 Heat the olive oil in a large skillet over medium-high heat until just about to smoke. Add the steak tips and cook for 5 to 6 minutes, until browned on all sides. Transfer to a plate and tent loosely with aluminum foil.

4 Reduce the heat to medium and add the shallot to the skillet. Cook, stirring, for 1 to 2 minutes, until tender and starting to brown. Add the balsamic vinegar and honey. Increase the heat to medium-high and simmer for 3 to 4 minutes, until reduced by half. Return the steak tips to the pan, along with any juices that have accumulated on the plate, turning them in the glaze. Serve with the Roasted Fingerling Potatoes and Creamed Spinach alongside, topped with a little pat of the compound "butter."

ROASTED FINGERLING POTATOES

1 pound fingerling potatoes
2 tablespoons olive oil
¼ teaspoon kosher salt
2 teaspoons chopped fresh rosemary
4 cloves garlic, finely minced or pressed

Preheat the oven to 425°F. Combine all the ingredients in a bowl, tossing well to coat. Transfer to a small baking dish or roasting pan, using a rubber spatula to scrape out all of the olive oil and seasonings onto the potatoes. Roast for 25 minutes, until golden brown, tossing a couple of times.

. . . continued

CREAMED SPINACH

2 tablespoons olive oil

½ cup diced yellow onion

2 tablespoons superfine brown rice flour

1¼ cups rice milk, warmed

1 pound fresh baby spinach

Big pinch of ground nutmeg

Freshly ground pepper

¼ teaspoon salt

¼ cup shredded Daiya vegan cheddar

1   In a medium-size pot, heat the olive oil over medium heat. Add the onion and cook, stirring often, for 6 minutes, until starting to brown.

2   Add the brown rice flour and cook for 2 minutes, stirring constantly, until golden and aromatic. Add the warm rice milk, stirring constantly. Bring to a simmer; reduce the heat to medium-low and cook for 5 minutes to thicken up a bit, stirring often.

3   Meanwhile, bring a large pot of water to a boil and steam or blanch the spinach until just wilted and dark green, about 3 minutes. Transfer to a colander, run under cold water to stop the cooking, and squeeze out any excess liquid. Pulse in a food processor until coarsely chopped, about 15 pulses, or chop coarsely by hand.

4   Add a big pinch of nutmeg to the rice milk mixture, along with a few turns of pepper and the salt. Add the vegan cheddar and cook, stirring often, for 2 minutes, until the cheese is starting to melt. Add the chopped spinach and cook until heated through and creamy, about 2 minutes more. Serve hot!

Chimichurri Flank Steak

Flank steak is a highly flavorful cut of meat that lends itself well to the sassy Argentine herbal chimichurri sauce, and pairs beautifully with potatoes. I also like to serve this steak with steamed broccoli.

SERVES 4

1½ **pounds trimmed flank steak**
¾ **teaspoon salt**
½ **teaspoon ground cumin**
½ **teaspoon ground coriander**
¼ **teaspoon freshly ground pepper**
1 **small clove garlic**
¼ **cup chopped yellow onion**
⅛ **teaspoon cayenne pepper**
½ **cup chopped parsley**
¼ **cup chopped cilantro**
1 **tablespoon rice vinegar**
¼ **cup extra virgin olive oil**
   Baked potatoes for serving (see note)
   Steamed broccoli for serving
   (see headnote, page 33)

1   Preheat the broiler on high.

2   Pat the steak dry. Combine ½ teaspoon of the salt with the cumin, coriander, and black pepper. Rub this mixture on both sides of the steak and broil the steak on the broiler pan about 4 inches from the heat source for 6 minutes per side for medium-rare. Transfer to a cutting board and let rest for 5 minutes.

3   Meanwhile, pulse the garlic in a food processor with the blade attachment until finely minced. Add the onion and cayenne pepper. Pulse until the onion is finely minced. Add the parsley and cilantro and pulse until finely chopped, then add the vinegar and the remaining ¼ teaspoon salt. Pulse; then, with the food processor running, drizzle in the olive oil a little at a time until you have a nice creamy herb sauce.

4   Cut the steak into thin slices, holding the knife at a 45-degree angle. Serve with the sauce, baked potatoes, and steamed broccoli.

Note: To make speedy baked potatoes, wrap each of the baking potatoes in a dampened paper towel. Cook in the microwave, either using the sensor for baked potatoes or for 12 minutes on high. Let rest for 5 minutes before serving.

Stuffed Peppers

Stuffed peppers make a great holiday or party dish. So pretty and festive, they are also packed full of savory goodness. Additionally, each little pepper half is a balanced bite, with protein, whole-grain carbs, and veggies.

SERVES 4

4 red bell peppers, sliced in half vertically, stems kept intact, and seeded (see note)

1 tablespoon olive oil

$1/2$ cup chopped yellow onion

3 cloves garlic, minced fine or pressed

1 pound sweet Italian sausage, casings removed (see note, page 38)

1 tablespoon red wine vinegar

1 cup diced canned tomatoes
Freshly ground pepper

1 cup cooked long grain brown rice (try Lundberg Ready Rice)

$1/4$ cup chopped fresh parsley

1 cup shredded Daiya vegan pepperjack
Sweet paprika for garnish

1   Adjust the oven rack to the top third of the oven and preheat the broiler on high. Line a baking tray with aluminum foil.

2   Put the bell pepper halves into a microwave-safe container, cover, and heat for 3 to 4 minutes, until tender. They can overlap. Remove from the microwave and lay out on the prepared baking tray, cut side down. Pat the backs slightly with paper towels to dry, then spray the peppers with cooking spray. Broil 6 inches from the heat source for 6 to 7 minutes, rotating the pan once halfway through, until black spots are starting to appear on the peppers. Remove from the oven and set aside.

3   Meanwhile, heat the olive oil in a large heavy pan over medium heat. Cook the onion for 2 minutes, until tender, stirring a few times. Add the garlic and cook for 1 minute more, stirring. Increase the heat to medium-high and add the sausage, breaking it up into crumbles with a spoon or spatula, and cooking until no longer pink, about 5 minutes. Add the red wine vinegar and cook for 1 minute, stirring a few times. Add the tomatoes, season with a few turns of pepper, add the rice, and heat through for about 2 minutes. Stir in the parsley and $1/2$ cup of the vegan pepperjack.

4   Flip the pepper halves so they are cut side up. Spoon the sausage filling gently into them, filling until they are heaping and slightly mounded. Sprinkle the remaining $1/2$ cup vegan pepperjack evenly over the peppers, sprinkle the tops with a little paprika, and broil for 4 minutes more, until the tops are turning spotty brown. Serve hot!

Note: When halving the peppers, use a sharp knife and make sure each half still retains its share of the stem. This will help the peppers hold their shape once they're stuffed. Gently remove the seeds.

Center-Cut Pork Chops with Apricot Glaze and Roasted Brussels Sprouts

"Pork chops and apricots" rolls off the tongue just as smoothly as "pork chops and applesauce"—and it's equally delicious. It just may be the new normal! Look for frenched center-cut chops if you can find them. Bone-in chops stay a lot more succulent.

My son Lennon, who is a finicky eater, has an unexpected love of roasted brussels sprouts, and eats them like there's no tomorrow. If you have a sprout lover like Lennon in your house, you may want to double the following recipe. Around Thanksgiving, the full sprout stalks start showing up in the grocery store. These will be your freshest option, as you literally just cut the sprouts off the stalk. One large stalk usually has about 2 pounds of sprouts on it—enough to serve eight people.

SERVES 4

4   (8-ounce) bone-in center-cut pork chops
Salt and freshly ground pepper
½   cup apricot jam
2   tablespoons Dijon mustard
1   teaspoon chopped fresh thyme
2   tablespoons olive oil
2   teaspoons balsamic vinegar
Roasted Brussels Sprouts (recipe follows)

1   Rinse the chops and pat them dry, or use a knife to scrape the surfaces clean (my mother does it this way). Sprinkle both sides with salt and pepper.

2   In a small bowl, combine the jam, mustard, and thyme, stirring well.

3   Heat the olive oil in a large heavy pan over medium-high heat. Once it starts to shimmer, add the chops and cook for 4 to 5 minutes per side, until browned and cooked through. Transfer to a plate and cover with tented foil.

4   Reduce the heat to low and add the jam mixture to the pan, stirring a couple of times with a wooden spoon to incorporate; add the vinegar and cook, stirring and scraping up any browned bits on the bottom of the pan, for about 1 minute or until the glaze has thickened up. Return the chops to the pan, adding back any juices that have run off, and turn the chops in the glaze. Transfer the chops to serving plates and spoon more glaze over the chops. Serve with the Roasted Brussels Sprouts.

. . . continued

ROASTED BRUSSELS SPROUTS

1   pound brussels sprouts (preferably small ones)
2   tablespoons olive oil
$\frac{1}{2}$ teaspoon kosher salt
$\frac{1}{8}$ teaspoon freshly ground pepper

1   Preheat the oven to 450°F. Line a baking tray with aluminum foil.

2   Trim the ends of the sprouts if they are browned, and get rid of any yellow leaves. Toss the sprouts well with the olive oil, salt, and pepper. Transfer to the prepared baking tray, using a rubber spatula to scrape out the last of the olive oil, salt, and pepper.

3   Roast in the center of the oven for 25 minutes, shaking the tray a few times, until browning and crispy on the outside. Watch out, they are hot, hot, hot!

Cherry Pork Tenderloin Medallions with Butternut Squash

Pork tenderloin is a lean alternative to the endless amounts of chicken we eat in my house. This dish is a personal favorite of mine. I have always loved pork combined with fruit, and the creamy butternut squash is my idea of heaven. Put the two together and you've got a crave-worthy supper that seems fancy, but really took you less than 30 minutes to whip up. Shh . . . nobody has to know.

SERVES 4

BUTTERNUT SQUASH

- 2 pounds 1-inch-cubed butternut squash
- 3 tablespoons plain vegan yogurt
- 2 tablespoons olive oil
- 1/2 teaspoon salt
- Pinch of cayenne pepper

PORK TENDERLOIN

- 1 1/2 pounds pork tenderloin, cut into 1-inch-thick slices
- Salt and freshly ground pepper
- 2 tablespoons olive oil
- 1/2 cup whole fruit cherry jam (there should be chunks of cherry in the jam)
- 1/4 cup Dijon mustard
- 2 tablespoons port

1 To make the squash, cook the squash in a covered microwave-safe dish in the microwave for 10 minutes, until tender. Drain, and puree in the food processor with the yogurt, olive oil, salt, and cayenne. Set aside, covered. Alternatively, you can puree with a handheld immersion blender.

2 While the squash is cooking, season the pork medallions with salt and pepper.

3 Heat the olive oil in a large pan over medium-high heat until starting to ripple and just about to smoke. Add the medallions and cook for 3 minutes per side, until browned. Mix the jam and mustard together and spoon over the pork. Reduce the heat to low and simmer, covered, for 15 minutes, turning the medallions every so often and spooning the sauce over the tops.

4 Transfer the pork medallions to a plate and tent with foil. Add the port to the cherry mixture in the pan, increase the heat to medium, and simmer to reduce to the consistency of a nice rich gravy, about 3 minutes. Return the medallions to the pan and turn in the sauce. Spoon the butternut squash onto the plates, top with the medallions, and spoon the sauce over the tops.

Crispy "Parmesan" Black Pepper Pork Cutlets with Asian Pear Salad

Like a peppery schnitzel, these black pepper pork cutlets are a revelation: crunchy, crispy, flavorful, and sure to become a family favorite. The cool, crisp, sweet Asian pear is the perfect complement to the savory cutlets.

SERVES 4 TO 6

¼ cup cornstarch or tapioca starch

¾ cup gluten-free breadcrumbs (preferably Ener-G)

¾ cup shredded Daiya vegan mozzarella

1½ teaspoons pepper

½ cup olive oil, plus more as necessary

2 tablespoons rice milk

1 pound thin pork cutlets (¼ inch thick)
   Salt

ASIAN PEAR SALAD

1 (5- to 6-ounce) bag mixed baby greens (I like the spicy mix)

1 Asian pear, cored and cut into thin slices (chilled is yummy!)

3 tablespoons olive oil

1 tablespoon freshly squeezed lemon juice

1 Pour the cornstarch into a shallow dish and set aside.

2 In another shallow dish, combine the breadcrumbs, vegan mozzarella, and ¾ teaspoon of the pepper. Toss well and set aside.

3 In a third shallow dish, whisk ¼ cup of the olive oil into the rice milk, 1 tablespoon at a time, until you have a creamy emulsion; this is your mock egg.

4 Rinse the pork cutlets and pat them dry. Sprinkle with salt. Turn each cutlet in the cornstarch, coating both sides, then dip in the mock egg mixture, then turn in the breadcrumb mixture, using your fingers to really adhere the breading to the cutlets.

5 Heat the remaining ¼ cup olive oil with the remaining ¾ teaspoon pepper in a large heavy pan or Dutch oven over medium-high heat until starting to shimmer. Cook half the cutlets in the oil, 3 minutes per side, until golden brown and crispy. Transfer from the pan to a platter lined with paper towels. Repeat with the remaining cutlets, adding more olive oil as necessary.

6 To make the salad, in a bowl, toss the baby greens with the Asian pear slices. In a small bowl, whisk together the olive oil and lemon juice, drizzle over the salad, and toss gently. Serve with the cutlets.

Garam Masala Lamb Chops with Cumin Quinoa

Garam masala is one of the most versatile Indian spice blends. It is fantastic with lamb or chicken. I recommend Spicely's organic garam masala, which is made in a dedicated allergen-free, gluten-free facility, and has amazing depth of flavor and an enticing aroma. I included this recipe for my husband, who loves chops. Between the lamb and the quinoa, it's a super-high protein meal, making it a great choice for anyone who's growing or trying to put on muscle. Pair it with a light salad or steamed veggies.

SERVES 4

- 2 cups low-sodium chicken broth
- 1 cup quinoa, rinsed
- 1 teaspoon ground cumin
- 1/2 teaspoon ground coriander
- 3/4 teaspoon salt
- 1/4 cup chopped jarred roasted red peppers (preferably Mediterranean or Turkish)
- 1 tablespoon garam masala
- 1/4 teaspoon pepper
- 5 teaspoons olive oil
- 8 (4-ounce) lamb loin chops

1   In a medium pot, combine the chicken broth, quinoa, cumin, coriander, 1/4 teaspoon of the salt, and the roasted peppers. Bring to a boil over medium-high heat, reduce the heat to a simmer, and cook, covered, for 15 minutes, until all the liquid is absorbed

2   In a small bowl, combine the garam masala with the remaining 1/2 teaspoon salt and the pepper.

3   Drizzle 1/4 teaspoon of the olive oil over each chop. Sprinkle the chops with half the spice rub, using your fingers to press the rub into the chops. Flip the chops and drizzle 1/4 teaspoon more of the olive oil on the other sides, then sprinkle with the remaining spice rub.

4   Heat the remaining 1 teaspoon olive oil in a large heavy pan (I use my large cast-iron skillet) over medium-high heat until almost smoking. Add the chops and cook for 4 to 5 minutes per side, until a nice brown crust forms on both sides. Transfer to a platter. Serve with the quinoa.

Lamb Kofta Kebabs

Lamb is a lovely alternative to beef, and is generally considered the least allergenic meat. Lamb kofta kebabs are a flavorful, kid-friendly way to serve lamb, and are very easy to make. Traditional recipes rely on allergenic pistachios and egg white, but I use hemp seeds and no egg. Look for roasted red bell peppers in the aisle with canned and jarred vegetables; for this recipe, drain the roasted peppers on paper towels before you chop them, or they'll be too soupy. The citrusy spice sumac is a fantastic way to reduce sodium content in a dish. It adds a big flavor boost, and is also a great substitute for lemon for those with citrus allergies. Mediterranean cultures have used it for centuries in place of lemon when lemons aren't in season. If truth be told, I often prefer it. Look for it in the spice aisle, as well as Aleppo pepper, a fruity, moderately spicy pepper that's milder than crushed red pepper flakes and has a hint of raisinlike flavor. In this dish, it flavors the lamb and the yogurt you serve it with, and its acidity mellows thinly sliced onion into a surprisingly delicious condiment. Serve these kebabs with basmati rice or the suggested flat bread. Or both!

SERVES 4

RED ONION WITH SUMAC

- 1 red onion
- 1 tablespoon ground sumac

LAMB KOFTAS

- 1 pound ground lamb
- ½ cup finely minced roasted red bell pepper (drained on paper towels before mincing)
- ½ teaspoon ground cumin
- ½ teaspoon dried oregano, crushed to a powder between your fingers
- ½ teaspoon dried spearmint, crushed to a powder between your fingers
- ¼ teaspoon ground Aleppo pepper, ancho chile powder, or ground chile flakes
- ⅛ teaspoon freshly ground pepper
- ¼ teaspoon salt
- 2 teaspoons ground sumac
- ½ cup shelled hemp seeds

- 1 (6-ounce) container plain vegan yogurt pinch of ground sumac
- 4 allergy-friendly flat breads or gluten-free tortillas

- 8 romaine hearts
- 1 large tomato, diced
  Fresh spearmint leaves, coarsely torn

1 To make the red onion, with a very sharp knife, slice the onion in half, then into quarters, then into the thinnest possible half-moons. Combine with the sumac, tossing well to coat. Set aside while preparing the kebabs.

2 To make the koftas, combine the lamb with the minced roasted bell pepper, cumin, oregano, spearmint, Aleppo pepper, black pepper, salt, and sumac in the bowl of a stand mixer fitted with the paddle attachment. Beat on medium speed until the meat becomes creamy and a little sticky, about 5 minutes. You can also do this in a food processor, pulsing it until the meat becomes smooth. Add the hemp seeds and mix until combined.

. . . continued

3   Heat a gas grill on high. You can also use a stovetop grill pan over high heat.

4   Use a rubber spatula to transfer the lamb to a work surface. Divide it into 8 portions and roll them into balls. If you wet your hands slightly with cool water, it will simplify the process. Mold the balls into 3$^1/_2$ by 1$^1/_2$-inch patties.

5   You can cook the koftas on metal skewers or not. If using them, use one skewer per patty. Skewer each patty and use your fingers to press the meat around the skewer. Don't worry if it's a little loose at first, it will tighten up as it cooks.

6   Spray the grill grates with cooking spray or brush with oil. Grill the koftas for 4 minutes per side, until browned, then for 30 seconds on each of the remaining uncharred edges.

7   Transfer the koftas to a platter. In a small bowl, sprinkle the yogurt with the pinch of sumac. Serve the lamb with the flat breads, red onion with sumac, romaine hearts, tomato, fresh mint, and yogurt.

Glazed Grilled Lamb Skewers

This beautiful dish is great as a summer party supper or a special family meal. Nobody will ever guess how little effort it actually took.

SERVES 4

2 pounds lamb, cut into 2-inch cubes (leg of lamb is good for this)

2 ripe but firm peaches, halved, then quartered, for a total of 8 chunks per peach

1 cup molasses

5 tablespoons Dijon mustard

2 tablespoons cider vinegar

4 cloves garlic, finely minced or pressed

½ teaspoon cayenne pepper

Salt and freshly ground pepper

1 tablespoon freshly squeezed lime juice

2 tablespoons olive oil

5 to 6 ounces baby arugula

1   Using four 14-inch metal skewers, thread each alternately with 5 pieces of lamb and 4 pieces of peach, starting and ending with lamb. Set the skewers on a large platter or plate.

2   In a small bowl, combine the molasses, mustard, vinegar, garlic, and cayenne, and season with salt and pepper. Stir well.

3   In another small bowl, whisk together the lime juice and olive oil. Add 2 tablespoons of the molasses glaze. Whisk well and set aside.

4   Pour the remaining glaze over the lamb skewers, turning to coat them well on all sides. Use a spoon if necessary to coat the meat and fruit evenly with glaze.

5   Heat a gas grill on high. When it's hot, spray the grill grates with cooking spray or brush with oil. Transfer the skewers to the grill, reserving the leftover glaze. Grill for 4 minutes, then brush with some of the reserved glaze. Flip the skewers and grill for 4 minutes more, brushing with a little more glaze. Flip again and grill for 4 minutes more, until the lamb is cooked through but still pink in the center, and browned on all sides. Don't overcook! Better to be underdone—you can always throw it back on for a minute or two more. Transfer the skewers to a serving platter.

6   Toss the arugula with the lime dressing. Adjust the salt and pepper to taste. Serve with the skewers.

TAKEOUT
at
HOME

Navigating your own allergy-free kitchen has become much easier over the past few years with the help of food allergy labeling and many more allergy-friendly products being offered. Even going out to dinner has become increasingly possible with the new food allergy awareness and training going on in culinary schools and many restaurants around the country. But takeout from your local fast food joint or diner is still a bit of a challenge. They just don't have the resources or training (yet) to have separate areas and equipment within one tiny kitchen to prevent the risk of cross-contact. Everything is fried in one deep fryer, or grilled on one grill. It's not feasible to ask for the taco stand operating out of your local car wash (yes, we have that in Los Angeles!) to make you a taco that's guaranteed to be free of dairy, gluten, tree nuts, peanuts, fish, shellfish, soy, or sesame. Or to ask your local diner to make you a burger that has absolutely no risk of dairy traces.

However, my kids, like most kids, want fast food and takeout more than any other type of food. They want chicken nuggets, Buffalo wings, tacos, pizza, and burgers, as do most of us, I'd venture to guess. The solution, if you want it truly allergy-free, is to make it yourself!

The following collection of recipes reads like the menu from the food court at your local mall. However, they are all allergy-free, and much healthier than anything you'd find at the food court. I use organic ingredients, no trans fats, low sodium, no lard, and no MSG. Get ready for fresh, fast food, takeout style, made right at home.

Buffalo Wings with Ranch Dressing

Buffalo wings are usually dependent on peanut oil, butter, and creamy ranch or blue cheese dressing; this allergy-free version is tangy, crispy, and succulent—perfect for game night, or a barbecue, or, in my house, any time my kids chant, "We want hot wings!" I've given proportions for four as a main dish, but it also serves eight as an appetizer. While deep-frying might seem horrifying, rest assured that the chicken actually absorbs very little oil, because it's not battered.

I've been working on a proper ranch dressing for the past year. To my chagrin, I'd gotten it almost right, but still not quite thick enough, until I made the wondrous discovery that several companies have launched soy-free vegan mayonnaise! Ta da! Ranch dressing that lacks for nothing. It's great with cut-up veggies for dunking.

SERVES 4

$3^{1}/_{2}$ **pounds chicken wings**
4   **cups canola oil**
    Salt and freshly ground pepper
$^{1}/_{4}$ **cup Earth Balance soy-free buttery spread**
$^{1}/_{4}$ **cup Louisiana hot sauce**
1   **tablespoon white vinegar**
    Ranch Dressing (recipe follows)
    Celery sticks

1   Rinse the wings under cold water and pat dry. Cut off the wing tips. Cut the wing in two at the joint; a cleaver works well for this (or you can ask the butcher to pre-cut them).

2   Heat the oil in a large, deep 10-inch pot, such as a Dutch oven, over high heat, to 400°F on a candy or oil thermometer.

3   Sprinkle the wings with salt and pepper and add half of the wings to the oil with tongs, using the tongs to stir and submerge all the wings. Don't worry; they can be a bit crowded. Cook, stirring occasionally with the tongs, for 10 to 11 minutes, until deeply golden and crispy. Remove from the oil, and drain on a paper towel–lined platter. Repeat with the second batch of wings.

4   Meanwhile, make the wing sauce by melting the buttery spread in a small pot over medium heat. Add the hot sauce and vinegar, bring to a simmer, and remove from the heat.

5   Put the wings on a platter and spoon the sauce over them. Serve with the Ranch Dressing and celery sticks.

. . . continued

RANCH DRESSING

- ½ cup rice milk
- 2 teaspoons freshly squeezed lemon juice
- 1 small clove garlic, finely minced or pressed
- 1 tablespoon finely chopped fresh parsley
- 1 tablespoon finely chopped celery leaves
- ¾ cup vegan soy-free mayonnaise
  or Rice Milk Mayonnaise (page 135)
- 1 teaspoon Dijon mustard
- ¼ teaspoon xanthan gum
- ¼ teaspoon salt
  Freshly ground pepper

In a small bowl, combine the rice milk with the lemon juice. In a blender or mini chopper, combine the garlic, parsley, celery leaves, vegan mayonnaise, and mustard. Pulse a few times. Add the rice milk mixture, and pulse. Add the xanthan gum and blend well. Add the salt and pepper to taste and blend until rich and creamy. You will have about 1¼ cups. Store in the fridge in an airtight container for up to a week.

Twice-Baked Potatoes

My son Monte calls these "the best thing ever!" He has no idea that they are stuffed with anything other than potato, and I'm not telling! To make them vegan, just skip the bacon.

3 large russet potatoes
1 (10-ounce) bag frozen cauliflower
3 slices bacon (optional)
1/4 cup Earth Balance soy-free buttery spread
2 tablespoons plain vegan yogurt
1/2 teaspoon salt
1 cup shredded Daiya vegan cheddar
   Minced fresh chives (optional)

1   Scrub the potatoes clean and pat dry. Prick with a fork a few times, put in a microwave-safe container, cover, and microwave for 12 to 16 minutes, until tender. (If you have a baked potato sensor setting, use that.) Let rest, covered, for a few minutes to finish cooking.

2   Meanwhile, put the cauliflower in a small pot, add water to cover the cauliflower halfway, and bring to a boil over high heat. Cover and cook for 3 minutes, until tender. Remove from the heat, drain, and puree in a food processor.

3   Chop the bacon and cook it in a heavy nonstick pan until crispy, about 5 minutes. Drain on paper towels.

4   Preheat the broiler on high.

5   Slice the potatoes in half lengthwise. If the potatoes are still too hot to handle, use a kitchen towel or an oven mitt to hold a potato half in one hand and gently scoop out the center into a medium bowl, leaving about 1/2 inch of potato in the skin so you have a solid "boat." Don't worry if the skin breaks a bit: the filling will help it adhere back together. Repeat with the other potato halves.

6   Use a handheld electric mixer to whip the potato in the bowl until fluffy. The potato will be a bit crumbly, but don't be tempted to overbeat, or it will turn to paste. Add the buttery spread and yogurt and mix. Add the cauliflower puree and salt, and then stir in 1/2 cup of the vegan cheddar.

7   Spoon the filling back into the potato skins until they are heaping full. Sprinkle the tops with the remaining 1/2 cup vegan cheddar. Set the potatoes on a broiler pan and broil 6 inches from the heat source until the cheese is turning spotty brown and melting, about 6 minutes.

8   Serve sprinkled with the chives and bacon bits.

Chicken Nuggets and Sweet Potato Fries

What's happier than a happy meal with chicken nuggets and fries? An allergy-free happy meal with organic chicken nuggets and beta carotene–packed sweet potato fries, all with half the fat! Choice Batter, featured in this recipe, absorbs 50 percent less fat than traditional batter does.

The trick to these allergy-free nuggets is your food processor. I first learned about binding meat with itself instead of with eggs or breadcrumbs from Ana Sortun's fantastic cookbook Spice. She specializes in Eastern Mediterranean recipes, and teaches that kneading meat in the food processor causes the proteins to change, creating a creamier consistency that holds together beautifully, for tender, light patties, kebabs, and nuggets. Voila, all chicken, no allergens!

You don't need a deep fryer for this recipe, but you do need a candy thermometer. I have an inexpensive one that measures temperature for both candy and oil (see Resources). I've written the fries recipe to serve four 3-ounce portions; you can double the recipe if you'd like more.

SERVES 4

1   (12-ounce) bag sweet potato spears or 2 medium-size sweet potatoes, peeled, halved horizontally, and cut into $1/4$-inch spears
2   tablespoons olive oil
    Salt and freshly ground pepper
$1/4$ teaspoon garlic powder
$1/4$ teaspoon sweet paprika
1   pound chicken breast, cut into 1-inch chunks
3   cups canola oil
1   cup Choice Batter (see Resources)
6   tablespoons cold water
    Ketchup or other condiments of choice (optional)

1   Preheat the oven to 450°F. Line a baking tray with parchment paper.

2   Toss the sweet potatoes in the olive oil. Sprinkle with $1/2$ teaspoon of salt, $1/4$ teaspoon of pepper, and the garlic powder and paprika, and toss well. Spread on the prepared baking tray, being sure not to overcrowd. Bake for 20 to 25 minutes, shaking the tray a few times, until golden. (If you cook on the convection setting, the potatoes will cook faster.)

3   Meanwhile, add the chicken to the food processor, season with salt and pepper, and pulse until you have made a paste, about 100 quick pulses.

4   Wet your hands slightly with cool water and mold the chicken into $1^1/2$-inch balls. You will have about 20. Use the palm of your hand to press them down into nugget shapes.

. . . continued

5   Heat the canola oil in a large, deep, heavy pan over high heat until it reaches 375°F on a candy or oil thermometer.

6   Combine the Choice Batter with ¼ teaspoon of pepper in a wide dish or bowl. Whisk well. Pour in the cold water and stir until smooth. Let rest for 5 minutes.

7   Gently add half the nuggets to the batter, turning to make sure they are well coated. Test the oil for readiness by dropping in a tiny bit of batter; it should sizzle up fast.

8   Add some of the battered nuggets to the hot oil, being careful not to splatter yourself. Do not overlap them, or they'll stick together. Cook the nuggets for 5 to 6 minutes, turning halfway through, until deeply golden. Transfer with tongs to a paper towel–lined platter. Repeat with the remaining nuggets. Serve with ketchup or the condiments of your choice.

Black Bean and Cheese Quesadillas with Roasted Green Chiles

I make these for breakfast, lunch, and dinner. They couldn't be any easier. The special flavor boost is the fire-roasted green chiles, which are a Southwestern specialty. You can find them canned in most grocery stores along with the Mexican ingredients. They aren't spicy hot, just full of flavor, so they're kid-friendly, too!

SERVES 4

1 (15-ounce) can black beans, drained and rinsed

¼ teaspoon ground cumin

¼ teaspoon salt

¼ teaspoon freshly ground pepper

1 (4-ounce) can diced mild fire-roasted green chiles (about ¼ cup)

½ cup shredded Daiya vegan pepperjack

½ cup shredded Daiya vegan cheddar

½ cup shredded Daiya vegan mozzarella

¼ cup chopped cilantro

4 (12-inch) gluten-free tortillas
Chunky salsa for serving (optional)

1   Empty the black beans into a bowl and crush slightly with the back of a fork. Add the cumin, salt, and pepper and mix. Stir the in the green chiles. Add the vegan cheeses, toss, and then stir in the cilantro.

2   Spread a heaping ½ cup of filling over half of each tortilla in a half-moon shape, leaving a 1-inch border. Fold the other half over, and press down.

3   Put two quesadillas at a time in a large non-stick skillet (I use my 12-inch cast-iron skillet) over medium-high heat. Cook for 2 minutes, pressing down slightly with a spatula. Flip (see note below), and cook for 2 minutes more. Remove from the pan, and cut into halves. Repeat with the remaining two quesadillas. Serve with a little salsa on the side.

Note: To flip neatly, lift a quesadilla with a spatula, rotate the pan, and flip the quesadilla into the open spot, now properly positioned. Repeat the lift, pan rotation, and flip with the other quesadilla.

Pumpkin Enchiladas with Beans and Chicken

Mild but flavorful, this healthy dish is really hitting all the nutritional marks. Pick up chopped red onions and precut green bell pepper in the produce section to speed your prep. Use leftover chicken, shredded with two forks.

To soften your tortillas, place the stack between two sheets of paper towels and microwave for about 30 seconds, until just softened. I've created a mild recipe for kids' palates, but if you want it spicier, add some jalapeño to the filling or serve with pickled jalapeños and a chunky salsa.

SERVES 4

1 tablespoon olive oil
½ cup chopped red onion
⅓ cup minced green bell pepper
1 teaspoon chili powder
1 teaspoon ground cumin
⅛ teaspoon cayenne pepper
1 (15-ounce) can pumpkin
1½ cups chicken broth
¼ teaspoon salt
 Freshly ground pepper
1 (15-ounce) can kidney beans, drained and rinsed
¼ cup shredded Daiya vegan pepperjack
1 cup shredded cooked chicken
1 tablespoon freshly squeezed lime juice
8 (6-inch) corn tortillas
¼ cup shredded Daiya vegan mozzarella
2 tablespoons chopped cilantro

1   Preheat the oven to 400°F. Grease a 7 by 11-inch baking dish.

2   Heat the olive oil in a large pan over medium-high heat. Cook the onion and green bell pepper until slightly softened, 3 minutes. Add the chili powder, cumin, and cayenne pepper and cook for 30 seconds, stirring. Add the pumpkin, chicken broth, salt, and pepper. Heat through for a minute or so.

3   Pour the beans into a medium-size bowl and mash slightly with the back of a fork. Stir in the vegan pepperjack and 1½ cups of the pumpkin mixture. Add the chicken and lime juice and toss.

4   Fill each tortilla with a heaping ⅓ cup of filling. Roll, and place seam side down in the baking dish. You will be able to fit eight snugly. Spoon the remaining pumpkin mixture over the tops and sprinkle with the vegan mozzarella. Cover with aluminum foil. Bake for 10 minutes, covered. Remove the aluminum foil and bake for 10 minutes more. Serve sprinkled with a little cilantro.

Tacos

We like to have a taco night at least once a month. Not only are these tacos delicious, but they are also a million times healthier for you than traditional restaurant tacos, which are usually full of lard, MSG, any number of common allergens, and an excess of sodium. These are made with only 1 tablespoon of heart-healthy olive oil and my allergy-free homemade taco seasoning—you'll feel practically virtuous serving this fast food. Using beef will make for a more crumbly taco filling, which my kids prefer; bison or buffalo meat is very lean and super high protein; and my husband and I like ours best with dark meat turkey. Pick your protein to suit your family's palate. Use your Vidalia Chop Wizard (see page 23) with the finer grid to mince the onion and bell pepper in less than a minute.

SERVES 4

1   tablespoon olive oil
1   cup minced onion
2   cloves garlic, finely minced or pressed
1   cup minced green bell pepper
1   pound ground dark meat turkey, beef, or bison or buffalo
2   teaspoons chili powder
1   teaspoon smoked Spanish paprika
1/2   teaspoon ground cumin
3/4   teaspoon dried oregano
1/2   teaspoon salt
1/4   teaspoon freshly ground pepper
4   teaspoons red wine vinegar
1/4   cup tomato paste
2/3   cup water
1   tablespoon honey
8   corn taco shells or 6-inch soft corn tortillas
   Guacamole (optional)
   Shredded Daiya vegan cheddar (optional)
   Shredded lettuce
   Diced onions
   Diced tomatoes
   Chopped cilantro (optional)

1   Heat the olive oil in a large pan over medium-high heat. Add the onion, garlic, bell pepper, and turkey and cook, stirring, for 2 minutes, using a wooden spoon to break up the meat. Add the chili powder, paprika, cumin, oregano, salt, and pepper and cook for 3 minutes more, until the meat is no longer pink.

2   Add the red wine vinegar and stir a couple of times. Add the tomato paste, water, and honey. Bring to a simmer, and then cook over low heat, loosely covered, stirring occasionally, for 20 minutes more. In the last few minutes of cooking time, warm the taco shells.

3   Place the taco filling in a bowl, surrounded by bowls with guacamole, vegan cheddar, shredded lettuce, diced onion, diced tomatoes, and chopped cilantro, and have each diner prepare his or her own tacos.

Chicken Mole Soft Tacos

Mole is a chocolate-based sauce from Oaxaca, Mexico. It is traditionally dependent on peanuts or tree nuts, and sometimes sesame seeds, making this dish off-limits to those with nut and/or sesame allergies. But with the advent of sunflower seed butter, it is no longer forbidden. This recipe was taste-tested by my kids, who couldn't believe their luck at actually being allowed to eat chocolate for dinner! For the chocolate, I used half an Enjoy Life Dark Boom CHOCO Boom bar (see Resources). If you can't eat corn, swap brown rice tortillas for the corn tortillas. If you can't eat sunflower seeds, use pea butter instead (see Resources). Use rotisserie chicken for super speedy prep.

SERVES 4 TO 6

- 2 tablespoons canola oil
- 1/2 cup diced yellow onion
- 1 clove garlic, minced or pressed
- 2 tablespoons chili powder
- 1/4 teaspoon ground cinnamon
- 1 teaspoon ground cumin
- 1 teaspoon ancho chile powder
- 1 cup chicken broth
- 1 (15-ounce) can fire-roasted tomatoes
- 3 tablespoons raisins
- 2 tablespoons sunflower seed butter
- 1/2 teaspoon salt
- 3/4 ounce dark allergy-free chocolate
- 3 cups shredded cooked chicken
- 16 small (4 1/2-inch) soft corn tortillas
  Diced tomato (optional)
  Chopped onion (optional)
  Diced avocado (optional)
  Chopped cilantro

1   Heat the oil in a large heavy sauté pan over medium heat. Add the onion and garlic and cook, stirring often, for 2 minutes, or until slightly tender.

2   Add the chili powder, cinnamon, cumin, and ancho chile powder and cook for about 30 seconds more. Add the chicken broth, tomatoes, raisins, sunflower seed butter, and salt, and simmer for about 15 minutes over medium heat, stirring often. Add the chocolate, stir a few times to dissolve it, transfer the sauce to a food processor and puree. Return the sauce to the pan. Add the shredded chicken and stir, then bring to a simmer over medium heat, reduce the heat to low, and simmer for about 5 minutes, or until heated through.

3   Stack the tortillas between two paper towels and microwave for about 30 seconds to warm them.

4   To assemble, take a warmed tortilla, put about 2 tablespoons of chicken mole in the center, top with the garnishes of your choice, and add a sprinkle of chopped cilantro.

Note: Leftover chicken mole makes delicious burritos. Use large corn or brown rice tortillas. Fill each along the center horizontally with 2 tablespoons of warm rice and beans, then top with 2 tablespoons of warmed chicken mole and a little guacamole. Fold in both the left and right sides, fold up halfway from the bottom, roll up once more from the bottom to the top, and flip. The steam will seal the burrito.

Deep Dish Pizza with Italian Sausage

Deep dish gluten-free, allergy-free pizza? Really? Who would have thought it possible? Not me, until I had an inspiration: my biscuit recipe could easily be converted into a cornmeal crust. Aha! I worked hard on this recipe, in tribute to my husband, Adam, whose favorite food is deep dish pizza. We spent a few months living in Chicago during our first year of marriage, and he ate a lot of deep dish pizza back then. Whenever we are in Chicago, he still orders an entire pie for himself. But he's gluten-intolerant and mildly dairy-allergic, so it's some kind of masochism. This pizza is for my honey, and all you others out there who've been missing a deep dish pie!

While it may seem odd that I use the Daiya vegan cheddar in this recipe, trust me, it will produce the best results, flavorwise and texturally. The vegan mozzarella on top is just to keep up pizza appearances.

SERVES 4

2 cups Basic Gluten-Free Flour Mix (page 48) or Authentic Foods GF Classical Blend

2 tablespoons cornmeal

$\frac{1}{2}$ teaspoon xanthan gum

1 tablespoon baking powder

$\frac{1}{2}$ teaspoon salt

$\frac{1}{2}$ cup dairy-free, soy-free shortening, chilled

1 cup plain vegan yogurt

1 tablespoon rice milk

$\frac{2}{3}$ pound (2 links) Italian sausage, sweet or hot

$\frac{3}{4}$ cup pizza sauce

$\frac{1}{2}$ cup shredded Daiya vegan cheddar

$\frac{1}{4}$ cup shredded Daiya vegan mozzarella
   Dried oregano

1 Preheat the oven to 450°F. Grease an 8-inch round cake pan with shortening and sprinkle the bottom and sides with a little cornmeal, tapping out any extra.

2 In a large bowl, whisk together the flour mix, cornmeal, xanthan gum, baking powder, and salt. Add the shortening and use a pastry blender or two knives to cut it in until it has formed pea-size crumbs. You can also use your fingers to break up and work in the clumps of shortening if that's faster. Add the yogurt and use a rubber spatula to mix gently until just combined. Use the spatula to turn the dough into the prepared pan.

3 Flour your hands well and press the dough evenly into the bottom of the pan, using your thumbs to build the crust up the sides until it's just below the rim. You may have to flour your hands a few more times during this process to keep them from sticking to the dough. Don't worry if the dough seems thin; it will puff during baking.

4 Brush the crust evenly with the rice milk, using a pastry brush.

5   Bake in the center of the oven for 18 minutes, until starting to become golden.

6   Meanwhile, remove the sausage from the casings. Heat a nonstick skillet over medium-high heat. Add the sausage and cook for 8 minutes, breaking it up with a wooden spoon or spatula, until browned and crumbly.

7   Heat the pizza sauce in the microwave for 1 minute, until hot.

8   Remove the crust from the oven. Move the oven rack so it's in the top third of the oven, and preheat the broiler.

9   Spread the vegan cheddar in the bottom of the crust. Top evenly with the sausage. Spoon the sauce over the top of the sausage. Sprinkle with the vegan mozzarella and then with some oregano.

10   Broil the pie 6 inches from the heat source for 2 minutes, until the cheese is melting and the crust is deep golden brown. Keep a close eye on the pizza; some broilers are supercharged and will burn it in a matter of minutes. Cut into pie-shaped wedges and serve hot.

Pulled Barbecue Chicken Sandwiches with Classic Coleslaw

I have always loved pulled pork sandwiches, but the pork has to simmer slowly for hours to become tender. Not so with dark meat chicken! This pulled chicken is just as tasty, and it's better for you, too. It's great on a bun, garnished with bread-and-butter pickle chips, but equally yummy over quinoa or rice. In the words of my son Monte, "Yum!" I serve it with a creamy classic coleslaw made without the dairy, eggs, or soy in traditional versions.

To make the Rice Milk Mayonnaise used in the coleslaw, use a blender, not a food processor. The real trick to this recipe is the medicine dropper. I'm a mother of two young children, so this little tool is readily on hand. To emulsify the mayonnaise properly, you must drip the oil in a drop at a time, or it won't work. The best way to control the flow is with a dropper. It will take you a few minutes to get all that oil in the blender a drop at a time, but don't be tempted to rush it. Your patience will pay off with perfection. Who would have thought it possible? Egg-free, dairy-free, and soy-free mayonnaise, but still with a lovely buttercup hue and the lush creaminess of fresh mayonnaise. Feel free to add fresh herbs at the end, or to use all canola oil for a milder flavor.

SERVES 4

1   cup Quick and Easy Barbecue Sauce (page 92)
1   pound boneless, skinless chicken thighs, cut into 2-inch chunks
4   allergy-friendly hamburger buns (see Resources)
    Bread-and-butter pickle chips
    Classic Coleslaw (recipe follows)

1   Pour the sauce into a medium-size pot, bring to a simmer over medium-high heat, add the chicken, cover, reduce the heat to medium-low, and cook at a low simmer for 25 minutes, until cooked through.

2   Meanwhile, make the coleslaw.

3   Remove the chicken from the heat. Use two forks to shred the chicken. Don't rush it; it takes a few minutes. Toast or warm the buns. Divide the saucy chicken evenly among the buns. Serve topped with a couple of pickles, with the coleslaw on the side.

CLASSIC COLESLAW

- 6 tablespoons Rice Milk Mayonnaise (recipe follows) or vegan soy-free mayonnaise (see Resources)
- 2 tablespoons sugar
- 1/4 cup rice milk
- 2 tablespoons freshly squeezed lemon juice
- 1 tablespoon cider vinegar
- 3 cups shredded cabbage or 3 1/2 cups classic coleslaw mix
- 1/2 cup shredded carrot (omit if using the classic coleslaw mix)
- 2 tablespoons finely chopped onion
  Salt and freshly ground pepper

1   In a small bowl, whisk together the mayonnaise, sugar, rice milk, lemon juice, and vinegar.

2   Toss together the cabbage, carrot, and onion in a medium-size bowl. Add the dressing, toss well, season with salt and pepper to taste, cover, and refrigerate until ready to serve. Makes about 3 cups.

RICE MILK MAYONNAISE

- 1/3 cup rice milk, chilled
- 1 1/2 teaspoons freshly squeezed lemon juice
- 1/8 teaspoon ground white pepper
- 1 small clove garlic, pressed
- 1/4 teaspoon xanthan gum
- 6 tablespoons olive oil
- 6 tablespoons canola oil
- 1/2 teaspoon fine sea salt

1   Combine the rice milk with the lemon juice and white pepper in a blender. Add the garlic and the xanthan gum, and mix on high speed until foamy.

2   Set the blender on high and, using the medicine dropper, add the oils drop by drop through the hole in the lid of the blender until the mayonnaise begins to emulsify. (You may wish to use your other hand to cover most of the hole in the lid, to prevent splattering.) Take your time! Continue to add the oil in a steady drip until the mayonnaise is thick and creamy, scraping down the sides of the blender as necessary. (I turned my cheap old blender off several times to let it cool down while making this. You may also wish to take pauses.) Again, do not try to make this too quickly; the process of slowing incorporating the oil should take several minutes.

3   Add the salt, taste, and adjust the salt and lemon juice if desired.

4   Serve at room temperature; you'll have about 1 cup. Transfer any remaining mayonnaise to a jar and store tightly covered in the refrigerator for up to 1 week.

Out-N-In Burgers

One of the highlights of living in Southern California is In-N-Out Burger. These famous fast food burgers are known for their delicious special sauce and combo of tomato, iceberg lettuce, and sweet onion. But they are off-limits for those with dairy, egg, soy, or wheat/gluten allergies. I decided to remedy that for you, so that those with allergies (and those in other parts of the world) could still enjoy this awesome savory treat. You may wish to cut your burgers in half for kids; at In-N-Out they wrap them in a neat little packet to catch the sauce. This allergy-free burger is sure to make you feel out while you're in. Sliced Daiya vegan cheeses are available at the Whole Foods deli counter, and they are also now selling it in wedges.

SERVES 4

6 tablespoons Rice Milk Mayonnaise (page 135), or vegan soy-free mayonnaise (see Resources)

2 tablespoons ketchup

4 teaspoons sweet relish

1 teaspoon sugar

1 teaspoon cider vinegar

1 pound 85 percent lean ground beef

4 allergy-friendly hamburger buns (see Resources)

4 bun-size pieces iceberg lettuce

4 ($\frac{1}{4}$-inch-thick) slices ripe but firm tomato (preferably beefsteak)

4 ($\frac{1}{4}$-inch-thick) round slices sweet onion
Salt and freshly ground pepper

2 teaspoons canola oil

4 ounces Daiya vegan cheddar, thinly sliced

1 Preheat the oven to 400°F.

2 In a small bowl, combine the mayonnaise, ketchup, relish, sugar, and cider vinegar. Stir well until smooth, and set aside.

3 Mold the hamburger meat into four patties, each 4 inches in diameter and $\frac{1}{4}$ inch thick.

4 Bake the buns whole for about 2 minutes, until starting to brown on the outside.

5 Meanwhile, lay out the lettuce, tomato, and onion for easy burger assembly. Season the burger patties with salt and pepper.

6 Heat a large nonstick skillet over medium-high heat, add $\frac{1}{2}$ teaspoon of the canola oil, and heat until shimmering. Split 2 of the buns and add them to the pan cut side down. Cook the buns for 1 minute, until they are golden brown on the cut sides. Transfer them to a plate, add another $\frac{1}{2}$ teaspoon of canola oil to the pan, and repeat with the other 2 buns.

. . . continued

7   Heat ¹/₂ teaspoon more of the canola oil in the skillet. Add 2 of the burgers and cook for 2¹/₂ minutes without moving them, pressing down on them a few times with a spatula to press out some of the juices. Flip the burgers, press down firmly on each burger, and cook for 30 seconds. Top with 1 slice of cheese per burger, and cook for 2 minutes more. Transfer to a plate. Add the remaining ¹/₂ teaspoon canola oil to the pan and repeat with the remaining 2 burgers.

8   To assemble, spoon 1 heaping tablespoon of the special sauce onto each of the bottom buns, top with the tomato slices, iceberg lettuce, then burgers, then sweet onion slices, then top buns. I like a little extra special sauce on mine, but let your taste be the judge.

Sloppy Joes

Sloppy Joes hold a special place in my heart. I always looked forward to them at my elementary school cafeteria, because they were something my mother never made at home. I've flipped the situation in our house. I pack my kids' lunches, but make them Sloppy Joes at home. Sneaking a little grated carrot into these boosts the nutrients. Serve with more baby carrots for a double dose of beta-carotene and a nice side of crunch!

SERVES 6

2 tablespoons olive oil

1½ cups finely chopped onion

3 cloves garlic, minced or pressed

1¼ pounds ground beef or dark meat turkey

1½ teaspoons chili powder

1 teaspoon smoked Spanish paprika

½ teaspoon dried oregano
   Pinch of cayenne pepper

½ teaspoon salt

¼ teaspoon freshly ground pepper

½ cup grated carrot

1 tablespoon dark brown sugar

¾ cup ketchup

1½ cups crushed or pureed tomatoes

¼ cup water

6 allergy-friendly hamburger buns
   (see Resources), warmed

1   Heat the olive oil in a large heavy pan over medium-high heat until starting to shimmer. Add the onion and cook, stirring often, for 4 minutes, until softened. Add the garlic and cook, stirring, for 1 minute.

2   Add the ground meat, spices, herbs, salt, and pepper and cook, breaking the meat up into small crumbles with a wooden spoon, for 3 minutes, until the meat is no longer pink.

3   Add the carrot and cook for another 2 minutes, stirring once or twice. Sprinkle with the brown sugar, toss, and add the ketchup, tomatoes, and water. Bring to a simmer, reduce the heat to medium-low, and cook at a simmer, stirring occasionally, for 10 minutes.

4   To serve, pile the Sloppy Joe mixture onto the warmed hamburger buns.

Chicken Fried Rice

This recipe was one of the most fun I've ever developed. I like a good challenge, and this certainly was one. How to make fried rice without the following allergens: soy, gluten (in soy sauce), peanuts, tree nuts, eggs, or sesame? Also no fish or shellfish. What a conundrum. Additionally, I opted to make it without legumes. Okay, I thought. I could work around green peas and omit the eggs; I wouldn't include shrimp and would use canola oil instead of peanut oil and sesame oil. But what about the soy sauce?

Soy sauce provides the acidity and sweetness we so love in a stir-fry. No tamari either? And fish sauce is out, too? What's a cook to do?

At first, I tried substituting lemon juice and mirin, the sweet Japanese cooking wine made from rice. It was totally wrong, and lacked the earthy depth of soy sauce. So I thought about what else has that depth of flavor, that umami.

Beef stock and kombu are both deep flavors, so I decided to stick them together, add a little garlic and ginger and a little something to sweeten, reduce to condense the flavor—and voila, my mock soy sauce was born. It's going to open a whole new world of food to you. Asian food is heavily dependent on the flavor of soy sauce, so if you avoid soy and gluten, you've been out of luck—until now! Get ready to get your stir-fry on. (Or, if you'd rather not bother with making the sauce, you can use coconut amino acids instead.)

SERVES 4

4 tablespoons canola oil

2 teaspoons finely minced garlic

2 teaspoons finely minced fresh ginger

2 green onions, white and green parts, chopped

$\frac{1}{2}$ cup minced yellow onion

$\frac{1}{2}$ cup diced carrot

$\frac{1}{2}$ cup sliced water chestnuts

$\frac{1}{2}$ cup chopped asparagus (fresh or frozen)

1 teaspoon salt

8 ounces ground chicken

Freshly ground pepper

3 cups cold cooked rice (preferably day-old jasmine rice)

1 tablespoon Cybele's Soy-Free Soy Sauce (recipe follows) or coconut amino acids

1 Heat a nonstick wok over high heat, add 2 tablespoons of the canola oil, and heat until the oil is starting to ripple slightly and is almost smoking. Add the garlic and ginger, toss to coat in the oil, add the green onions and toss, and then add the onion. Cook, tossing often, for about 2 minutes, until the onion is soft and turning golden.

2 Add the carrot and water chestnuts and cook until the carrot is soft and the water chestnuts are turning golden, about 2 minutes. Add the asparagus and cook, tossing, for about 2 minutes more. Sprinkle the vegetables with $\frac{1}{2}$ teaspoon of the salt, tossing well to coat, then transfer to a bowl and set aside.

3   Heat 1 more tablespoon of canola oil in the wok, then add the ground chicken. Use your spatula or spoon to really break up the chicken until it's crumbly and browned nicely, about 4 minutes. Sprinkle with the remaining 1/2 teaspoon salt and a little bit of pepper. Toss well to coat, then transfer the chicken to the bowl with the cooked vegetables.

4   Add the remaining 1 tablespoon canola oil to the wok, heat, and add the rice and cook, tossing often, for 2 to 3 minutes, until the rice is glossy and aromatic. Drizzle the rice with the mock soy sauce and toss until well coated. Add back in the vegetables and chicken and cook, tossing well, until heated through. Remove from the heat and serve.

CYBELE'S SOY-FREE SOY SAUCE

2   cups beef stock
2   (2 by 3-inch) pieces kombu seaweed
2   teaspoons cider vinegar
4   teaspoons molasses
1   teaspoon finely minced garlic
1   teaspoon grated or finely minced ginger
     Freshly ground pepper

Combine the beef broth, kombu, cider vinegar, molasses, garlic, ginger, and a couple of turns of pepper in a small saucepan. Bring to a boil over medium-high heat. Reduce to a simmer and cook over low heat for 30 minutes, until reduced to about 1/4 cup. Strain through a fine-mesh sieve, let cool to room temperature, then store tightly covered in the refrigerator. Keeps for 1 week.

Mu Shu Pork

Pick up shredded cabbage, shredded carrots, peeled garlic cloves, ground pork, and chopped red onion to whip up this old-school classic in no time at all. Use a mini chopper for the garlic and ginger, and the only prep you're left with is slicing the shiitakes and snow peas. When I was a kid, this was my favorite Chinese (-American) dish. The Plum Sauce is optional, but I like the combo of a little spicy sweetness with my pork dishes.

.... SERVES 4

STIR-FRY SAUCE
- ½ cup vegetable broth
- 2 tablespoons Cybele's Soy-Free Soy Sauce (page 141) or coconut amino acids
- 2 tablespoons canola oil
- 1 tablespoon rice vinegar
- 1 tablespoon cornstarch or tapioca starch
- 1 teaspoon honey

- 1 tablespoon canola oil
- 8 ounces ground pork
- 1 cup chopped red onion
- 2 tablespoons minced or grated ginger
- 2 large cloves garlic, minced or pressed
- 1 cup thinly sliced shiitake mushrooms
- ½ teaspoon salt
- 3 cups shredded cabbage
- 4 ounces snow peas, sliced into thin slivers vertically
- 1 cup shredded carrot
- 2 green onions, white and green parts, chopped
- 12 (4½-inch) corn tortillas or rice paper wrappers
  Plum Sauce (recipe follows)

1 To make the stir-fry sauce, combine the sauce ingredients in a jar or small plastic container, cover tightly, and shake until the honey and tapioca starch are completely dissolved.

2 Heat the canola oil over high heat in a nonstick wok or large skillet until almost smoking.

3 Add the pork, onion, and ginger. Cook, stirring, for 3 minutes, until the pork is no longer pink and the onion is tender, being sure to break up the pork with a spoon so it browns into a nice crumble. Add the garlic and mushrooms and cook, stirring often, for 5 minutes more, until the mushrooms are starting to brown. Add the salt, and toss.

4 Add the cabbage, snow peas, carrot, and green onions. Cook, stirring, for 2 minutes. Add the stir-fry sauce and cook for 3 minutes more, stirring. Give it the full 3 minutes for the flavors to develop and meld, and for the sauce to thicken.

5 Serve with the tortillas or rice paper wrappers and the Plum Sauce.

PLUM SAUCE

- 1 cup plum jam
- ½ teaspoon garlic, finely minced or pressed
- 2 teaspoons minced or grated ginger
- 2 tablespoons cider vinegar
- ¼ teaspoon salt
- 1 tablespoon Sriracha or other chile-garlic sauce

Combine all the ingredients in a pot and bring to a simmer over high heat. Reduce to medium-low and cook for 5 minutes, stirring often. Let cool to room temperature. Puree in a blender. You will have about 1 cup; store covered in the refrigerator for several weeks.

VEGAN

I started my kitchen career back when I was a teenager and a vegetarian. In those days, vegetarian food was pretty dependent on cheese. And lots of butter. And also, often, eggs. Vegetarian cuisine has come a very long way in the past twenty years or so; for one thing, it has moved away from all that fat. Going allergy-free has inspired me to think vegan, not just vegetarian, what with one son having a dairy allergy and the other being allergic to eggs. Incidentally, my husband also has a dairy allergy that was finally diagnosed a few years ago, so cutting out dairy was truly a blessing in disguise for all of us.

I'm crazy about vegan food. If it were just me I was feeding, I'd probably go totally veg. I adore high protein grains like quinoa and millet and am a bean fanatic, as is my son Monte, whom I often call my little chickpea. If you can't eat legumes, try the stuffed acorn squash, the pumpkin risotto, and the veggie lo mein in this chapter. If you can eat beans, then go for broke and try the awesome quinoa chickpea lettuce cups or the black-eyed pea cakes.

ADDITIONAL VEGAN RECIPES AND DISHES WITH A VEGAN OPTION

Quinoa Chickpea Lettuce Cups

This light summery recipe is so speedy that you can both cook and eat it in under 30 minutes. It's a great way to use up leftover cooked quinoa, which I always seem to have. To spice things up, I use fire-roasted tomatoes with chiles, but let your taste be the guide.

SERVES 4

2   tablespoons olive oil
¼   cup minced yellow onion
1   teaspoon minced garlic
⅛   teaspoon cayenne pepper
1   teaspoon ground cumin
¼   teaspoon salt
1   (15-ounce) can fire-roasted tomatoes or diced tomatoes
1   (15-ounce) can chickpeas, drained and rinsed
1½   cups cooked quinoa
1   tablespoon freshly squeezed lime juice
¼   cup chopped cilantro
1   avocado, diced
12   large leaves Boston or butter lettuce

1   Heat the olive oil in a large heavy pan and sauté the onion over medium-high heat for 2 minutes, until tender and starting to turn golden. Add the garlic, spices, and salt, and cook for 1 minute more.

2   Add the tomatoes and chickpeas, bring to a simmer, reduce the heat to medium, and cook for 5 minutes more, stirring occasionally. Add the quinoa and cook for 5 minutes more. Remove from the heat, add the lime juice and cilantro, and stir. Add the avocado, stir gently, and adjust the salt to taste.

3   Serve warm or at room temperature with the lettuce leaves. Spoon about 2 tablespoons of filling into the center of each leaf, wrap, and eat.

Pumpkin Risotto

You can use either pumpkin or butternut squash for this risotto. Look for it already peeled and cubed in the produce section or in the frozen foods aisle.

You will notice that there is no cheese in this risotto. While I love the Daiya vegan cheeses (perhaps too much!), I prefer to make allergy-free risotto without it. Daiya is great in Mexican dishes, and even many Italian-style dishes, such as those with a tomato base, but the flavors just don't meld in this Northern Italian classic. So I created this recipe to be perfect without cheese, vegan or not. If you can eat cheese, then go for the king of all cheeses, and pass around the grated fresh Parmesan. To gild the lily, I sometimes add a little truffle salt, and transport my family to Tuscany.

.... SERVES 4 TO 6

- 1½ cups Arborio rice
- 4½ cups vegetable broth
- ¼ cup olive oil
- 1 tablespoon Earth Balance soy-free buttery spread
- 1 cup chopped onion
- 2 cloves garlic, finely minced or pressed
- ½ cup white wine
- 2 cups ½-inch diced pumpkin or butternut squash
- ¼ teaspoon salt
- ¼ cup chopped fresh parsley
  Salt and freshly ground pepper
  Truffle salt (optional)

1   Combine the rice with 3½ cups of the broth in a microwave-safe container. Cover and microwave for 12 minutes, until the rice is softened and most of the liquid is absorbed.

2   Meanwhile, heat the remaining 1 cup broth in a small pan over medium heat until just below a boil. Set aside.

3   In a large pot or Dutch oven over medium heat, heat the olive oil and buttery spread until starting to shimmer. Add the onion and cook, stirring often, for 2 minutes, until aromatic. Add the garlic and cook for 1 minute more. Add the wine and cook until reduced by half, about 2 minutes. Add the pumpkin, salt, and ½ cup of the hot broth. Cook, stirring occasionally, for 5 minutes.

4   Add the rice and 2 tablespoons of the parsley, reduce the heat to medium-low, and cook for 10 minutes more, stirring constantly, until the pumpkin is tender and the rice is al dente. Remove from the heat, stir in the remaining ½ cup of broth, and season with salt and pepper. Cover and let rest for 2 minutes.

5   Serve topped with the remaining 2 tablespoons chopped parsley and sprinkled with the truffle salt.

Stuffed Acorn Squash with Millet, Spinach, Cranberries, and Hemp Seeds

Who says millet is just for the birds? Not anymore, it's not! This old-world gluten-free grain is high protein and delicately flavored. It's the perfect stand-in for couscous if you cook it right. Read on for the most delicious stuffed squash, packed full of nutrients galore. And so easy! I was shocked by how much my kids loved this, and I will be making it in heavy rotation now.

SERVES 4

1/2 cup millet

1 1/2 cups water

2 small acorn squash, halved and seeded
Salt and freshly ground pepper

1 tablespoon olive oil

1/2 cup chopped sweet or yellow onion

2 large cloves garlic, minced or pressed

1/4 cup dried cranberries

1 (5- to 6-ounce) bag baby spinach

1 tablespoon cider vinegar

1 teaspoon sugar

1/4 cup shelled hemp seeds, toasted (see note)

4 heaping teaspoons fine gluten-free breadcrumbs (I like Ener-G for this)

4 heaping teaspoons Earth Balance soy-free buttery spread or olive oil

1   Combine the millet and water in a small pot over medium-high heat. Bring to a boil, reduce the heat to medium-low, and simmer, covered, for 18 minutes, until the water is absorbed. Don't stir the millet or it will become creamy. You want it to cook up like rice, and refraining from stirring will accomplish this.

2   Meanwhile, spray the insides of the acorn squash halves with cooking spray or brush lightly with olive oil. Sprinkle with salt and pepper. Place face down on a large microwave-safe dish (I just use the microwave tray). Cover (I use a large mixing bowl—it's okay if the squash halves have to overlap a bit) and cook for 16 minutes, or until the squash is tender.

3   Meanwhile, heat the olive oil in a large heavy pan over medium heat. Add the onion and cook for 2 minutes, until tender. Add the garlic and cranberries and cook, stirring, for 1 minute. Add the spinach and cook, stirring often, until wilted, 2 minutes. Add the vinegar and sugar, stir, and season with salt and pepper. Cook, stirring, for 1 minute. Remove from the heat and stir in the hemp seeds.

. . . continued

Quick Ratatouille

This super speedy version of the classic Provençal summertime dish is another way to make use of my favorite kitchen gadget, the Vidalia Chop Wizard (see page 23). Use it with the larger grid (½-inch dice) to prep your onions, eggplant, zucchini, and summer squash in record time. Just slice the zucchini and summer squash lengthwise into ½-inch pieces, then use the Chop Wizard to dice. Cut the eggplant into ½-inch rounds, and do the same. Voila—perfect little ½-inch cubes! After making this dish, I decided I prefer it to traditional ratatouille, which is often stewed to mush. It's pretty and delicate and perfectly cooked. Serve with quinoa or any other gluten-free grain you like.

SERVES 4

4 tablespoons olive oil

1 cup small-diced red onion

½ teaspoon salt

3 cloves garlic, minced or pressed

1 pound eggplant (about 1 medium), peeled, cut into ½-inch rounds, then diced into ½-inch pieces

8 ounces zucchini, cut into ½-inch pieces

8 ounces summer squash, cut into ½-inch pieces

½ teaspoon herbes de Provence (preferably Spicely brand)

2 (14.5-ounce) cans diced tomatoes
Freshly ground pepper

2 tablespoons chopped fresh basil

1 Heat 2 tablespoons of the olive oil in a large Dutch oven over medium-high heat. Add the onion and salt and cook until softened and starting to brown, about 3 minutes. Add the garlic and stir. Add the remaining 2 tablespoons olive oil and the eggplant and cook, stirring often, for 4 minutes, until the eggplant is softened.

2 Add the zucchini and squash and toss, add the herbes de Provence and stir, and add the tomatoes and a few turns of pepper. Bring to a simmer, reduce the heat to medium-low, and cook, covered, for 15 minutes, stirring occasionally, until the vegetables are tender and the sauce has thickened up a bit. Remove the lid and cook for about 1 more minute, stirring a few times. Remove from the heat and stir in the basil. Serve hot, cold, or at room temperature.

Malaysian Vegetable Curry

Pack speed into this simple aromatic recipe by buying chopped onions, precut carrot spears, and red pepper strips. Serve over white rice.

2 stalks lemongrass

2 tablespoons canola oil

4 small serrano chiles or green Thai chiles, seeded, white pith removed, and chopped

1 cup diced yellow onion

3 cloves garlic, minced or pressed

1 teaspoon ground turmeric

2 teaspoons ground coriander

2 teaspoons ground cumin

1 teaspoon salt

2 cups coconut milk

1 large Yukon Gold potato, skin on, diced into 1-inch chunks (1½ cups)

1 cup chopped carrot

1 (14-ounce) can baby corn, drained and rinsed

1 red bell pepper, seeded and cut into strips (1½ cups)

1 tablespoon freshly squeezed lime juice
White rice for serving

½ cup unsweetened shredded coconut, toasted (optional; see note)

1　Prepare the lemongrass by removing the dry outer leaves, then trimming the top and bottom ends. Cut each stalk into 3 pieces that are 3 inches long, for a total of 6 pieces. Set aside.

2　Heat the oil in a heavy skillet or casserole over medium-high heat. Add the chiles and onion and cook, stirring occasionally, for 2 minutes, until both vegetables are slightly softened and the onion is starting to brown. Add the garlic, turmeric, coriander, cumin, and salt. Cook, stirring, for about 30 seconds. Add the coconut milk and lemongrass, then the potato, carrot, baby corn, and red bell pepper. Bring to a simmer, reduce the heat to medium-low, and simmer, loosely covered, for 20 minutes, or until the potato and carrot are tender.

3　Remove from the heat, stir in the lime juice, and serve hot, over rice, sprinkled with the toasted coconut.

Note: To toast coconut, heat a small skillet over medium-high heat. Add the shredded coconut and cook, stirring, until it becomes aromatic and slightly golden, about 2 minutes. Remove from the heat.

Kasha Varnishkas

This is a simple old-world Eastern European dish—good Jewish comfort food. Kasha are buckwheat groats, and varnishkas are bow-tie pasta. Since nobody has yet come out with a gluten-free bow-tie pasta (that I know of), I subbed cute little corn/quinoa shells, with good results. In place of the egg traditionally used for toasting the kasha, I used a mixture of flaxseed meal and hot water—a "flax egg"—which worked just great. I also substituted olive oil for the traditional chicken fat (which my great-grandmother would have used) to keep it vegan and healthy. This dinner is packed full of fiber, good-for-you carbs, and protein-rich buckwheat and quinoa. It hits a nutritional home run!

SERVES 4 TO 6

1 tablespoon golden flaxseed meal

3 tablespoons hot water

1 cup buckwheat groats (kasha)

4 tablespoons olive oil

1½ cups diced yellow onion

8 ounces sliced or chopped mushrooms

2 cloves garlic, finely minced or pressed

2 cups vegetable broth
Salt and freshly ground pepper

1½ cups gluten-free corn/quinoa mini shells or other small short pasta of your choice

1 tablespoon Earth Balance soy-free buttery spread or olive oil

2 tablespoons balsamic vinegar

2 tablespoons chopped fresh parsley

1   In a bowl, combine the flaxseed meal and hot water, whisking to combine. Let it sit for about a minute to thicken. Add the buckwheat groats and toss to coat.

2   Heat 1 tablespoon of the olive oil in a heavy skillet over medium-high heat. Add the buckwheat groats and press down into the pan to form a single layer; it should make contact with the oil to brown the groats a bit. Cook, stirring often, then repeating the flattening motion, for 4 minutes, until the buckwheat is toasted and aromatic and the grains have separated again. Remove from the heat and set aside.

3   Bring a pot of water to a boil over high heat.

4   Heat the remaining 3 tablespoons olive oil in a large Dutch oven or other heavy pot over medium-high heat. Add the onion and mushrooms and sauté for 4 minutes, stirring often, until starting to brown. Add the garlic and cook for 1 minute more, stirring a few times. Add the broth and a big pinch of salt and a few turns of pepper. Bring to a boil. Add the buckwheat to the broth, reduce the heat to low, cover, and simmer for 14 minutes, until the buckwheat is tender.

5   Meanwhile, cook the pasta according to the instructions on the package. Drain, and combine with the buttery spread. Add to the pot with the cooked buckwheat. Drizzle in the balsamic vinegar and cook over medium heat, stirring, for 2 minutes, until the flavors meld and the balsamic has lost its tang. Stir in the parsley, and adjust the salt and pepper to taste.

Vegetable Lo Mein

This is a simple, healthy, colorful vegan version of a dish usually loaded with allergens, from gluten, to eggs, to soy, to peanuts, to sesame. It's top-eight-allergen-free, but tastes just like regular lo mein. Look for precut stir-fry vegetables in the produce section or in the frozen foods aisle. If you want, you can reduce the heat by cutting back on the red pepper flakes. The hemp seeds are a great finishing touch, but if you don't have them, no worries.

SERVES 4

8 ounces thin gluten-free spaghetti (I like Ancient Harvest for this)

1 cup mushroom broth

2 tablespoons coconut amino acids or Cybele's Soy-Free Soy Sauce (page 141)

2 teaspoons honey

1 tablespoon cornstarch or tapioca starch

½ teaspoon red pepper flakes

1 tablespoon canola oil

1 (16-ounce) bag fresh or frozen mixed stir-fry veggies

2 cups mung bean spouts

3 green onions, white and green parts, chopped

4 cloves garlic, minced or pressed

1 tablespoon finely minced ginger

½ teaspoon kosher salt

1 tablespoon toasted shelled hemp seeds (see note, page 150)

1   Bring a pot of water to a boil over high heat. Cook the pasta according to the instructions on the package until it is al dente. You want it a bit underdone, so keep a close eye on it. Drain and set aside.

2   Meanwhile, in a bowl, combine the mushroom broth, coconut amino acids, and honey. Whisk well to really dissolve the honey. Add the cornstarch and whisk until completely dissolved. Stir in the red pepper flakes. Set aside.

3   Heat a nonstick wok or large skillet over high heat. Add the oil, swirl it around, and heat until it's almost smoking. Add the mixed vegetables, bean sprouts, and green onions and cook, stirring, for 2 minutes. Add the garlic and ginger and cook, stirring, for 2 minutes more. Add the noodles and toss well with tongs. Sprinkle with the salt and cook a minute or so more, until heated through. Add the mushroom broth mixture and cook, stirring often, for 4 minutes, until the sauce has thickened.

4   Transfer the lo mein to a serving platter and serve topped with a sprinkling of toasted hemp seeds.

Portobello Shepherd's Pie

Portobello mushrooms are a nice meaty vegan alternative to traditional lamb or beef in shepherd's pie. Look for chopped red onion and precut carrot and celery sticks to speed your prep time. Or baby carrots work like a charm when diced in the Vidalia Chop Wizard (see page 23).

SERVES 4 TO 6

POTATO TOPPING

- 1 pound russet or other baking potatoes
- 1 pound orange sweet potatoes
- 3 tablespoons plain vegan yogurt
- 2 tablespoons olive oil
- 1/4 teaspoon salt
- 1/4 cup rice milk

FILLING

- 2 tablespoons olive oil
- 1/2 cup diced red onion
- 1 cup diced carrot
- 1 cup diced celery
- 3 medium or 2 large portobello mushroom caps, cut into 1/2-inch dice
- Salt and freshly ground pepper
- Big pinch of allspice
- 1 teaspoon dried thyme
- 2 tablespoons superfine brown rice flour
- 1 1/2 cups vegetable stock or mushroom broth
- 2 tablespoons tomato paste
- 1 tablespoon Pickapeppa Sauce or other hot sauce
- 1/2 cup frozen peas
- 1 tablespoon Earth Balance soy-free buttery spread or olive oil
- Sweet paprika

1   To make the topping, prick the potatoes and sweet potatoes a few times with the tines of a fork, put in a microwave-safe container, cover, and cook in the microwave on high for 10 to 12 minutes, until tender. (If you have a baked potato setting, use that.) Let rest in the microwave for 5 minutes, then remove one at a time and hold with a kitchen towel in one hand—they will be hot! Cut in half and spoon out the potato flesh into a medium-size bowl; discard the skins.

2   Add the yogurt, olive oil, salt, and rice milk to the potatoes in the bowl. Using a handheld electric mixer, whip until smooth. Set aside.

3   To make the filling, heat the olive oil in a large sauté pan over medium-high heat. Once the oil is hot and starting to ripple, add the onion, carrot, celery, and diced mushrooms. Sprinkle with salt and pepper and the allspice and thyme. Cook, stirring often, for 5 minutes, until tender. Sprinkle with the brown rice flour, reduce the heat to medium, and cook for 2 minutes, stirring often.

4   Add the vegetable stock, bring to a boil, and deglaze the bottom of the pan, scraping up any browned bits, for 1 minute. Add the tomato paste and Pickapeppa and cook, stirring, for 1 minute. Stir in the peas.

5   Preheat the broiler to high and grease a 7 by 11-inch broiler-safe casserole or baking dish.

6   Transfer the filling to the prepared casserole and top evenly with the mashed potatoes. Dot the top with the buttery spread and sprinkle with paprika. Broil 6 inches from the heat source for 6 minutes, until the top is browned. Keep a close eye on it so it doesn't burn.

Black-Eyed Pea Cakes with Mediterranean Salad

This is a vegan power meal, packed full of protein and fiber. Look for chickpea flour in the baking aisle at Whole Foods or at any Indian market. It's also called garbanzo bean flour or cece flour. It's the secret ingredient to this recipe (no longer secret).

SERVES 4

1 (15-ounce) can black-eyed peas, drained and rinsed

1 tablespoon olive oil

2 tablespoons lime juice

1/2 cup diced red bell pepper

1/2 cup chopped green onions, white and green parts

2 tablespoons chopped fresh parsley

1 cup chickpea flour

1 teaspoon ground cumin

1/8 teaspoon cayenne pepper

1/4 teaspoon freshly ground pepper

1/2 teaspoon salt

3/4 cup hot water

3 tablespoons canola oil
  Mediterranean Salad (recipe follows)

1 Empty the black-eyed peas into a mixing bowl. Using the back of a fork, smash them a bit against the side of the bowl, being sure to leave some whole. Combine with the olive oil, lime juice, bell pepper, green onions, and parsley. Set aside.

2 In another bowl, whisk together the chickpea flour, cumin, cayenne, pepper, and salt. Whisk in the hot water until smooth. Add the black-eyed pea mixture. Stir well.

3 Heat 2 tablespoons of the oil in a heavy nonstick skillet over medium-high heat (I use my trusty cast-iron pan). Scoop out a heaping 1/4 cup of batter per cake and cook for 4 minutes per side, until golden, adding the remaining canola oil, as necessary.

4 Season the cakes with salt and pepper to taste, and serve hot with the Mediterranean Salad on the side.

MEDITERRANEAN SALAD

....

½ English cucumber, cut into ½-inch pieces (1 cup)

1 cup cherry tomatoes, halved, or 1 cup tomatoes cut into 1-inch pieces

½ cup bell pepper cut into 1-inch pieces

8 kalamata olives

1 green onion, green and white parts, chopped

2 tablespoons freshly squeezed lemon juice

1 tablespoon extra virgin olive oil

¼ teaspoon dried oregano

Salt and freshly ground pepper

....

In a bowl, toss together the cucumber, tomatoes, and bell pepper. Add the olives and green onion and toss. Drizzle with the lemon juice and olive oil and sprinkle with the oregano and some salt and freshly ground pepper. Toss, and adjust the salt and pepper to taste. Makes about 2½ cups.

Acknowledgments

Cookbooks are always a collaboration between the author and the eaters. I'd like to thank all my taste-testers and champions; my husband Adam for his constant enthusiasm for everything I cook, my sous chefs and sons Lennon and Monte and their friends Domenic Smith and Christopher Kennedy who always clean their plates with gusto, my dear friends Deirdre Moncy and Brandi Smith for their support and feedback. Thank you to The Allergist Mom, Sarah M. Boudreau-Romano, MD, FAAP, for testing recipes and writing such a thoughtful foreword. Thanks to my agent, Mitchell Waters for his belief in the project and guidance throughout. Thanks to my editor Melissa Moore, who is a joy to partner with, to Chugrad McAndrews for his gorgeous photography, Karen Shinto for her brilliant food styling, and to Leigh Noe for her impeccable eye for prop styling and her amazing collection. Thanks to Gwen Smith from *Allergic Living*, Nicole Smith from *Allergic Child*, Lynda Mitchell from Kids with Food Allergies, Elana Amsterdam from Elana's Pantry, Aran Goyoaga from Cannelle et Vanille, and Peter Reinhart, master of bread, for reviewing the manuscript for me and offering kind words.

Thank you also to Alex Postman, former editor-in-chief of *Whole Living*, who was so supportive of me and my allergy-friendly recipes and offered me a place to develop earlier versions of a handful of what's now in this book.

Thanks to my parents, Eric Chivian and Susanna Deiss, my friends ("wine enthusiasts," you know who you are!), and my readers, many of whom have become my friends. Thanks to Eleanor Garrow for her dedication to food allergic children, and huge thanks to FAAN/FAI, and the entire food allergy community—we have made tremendous strides, and as our numbers have doubled in the past ten years, so too have our efforts to find a cure, to innovate, and to thrive. And thanks to my late mother-in-law, Wendy. I miss her terribly, and again, thank her for giving me my very first Vidalia Chop Wizard and starting me down the path to free and easy cooking. And one last thank you . . . thanks to all of you who are reading this and are taking the time to make these recipes for yourselves and your loved ones. Big thanks!

Resources

SAFETY NOTE:

Because each person's food sensitivities and reactions are unique, ranging from mild intolerance to life-threatening and severe food allergies, it is up to you to monitor ingredients and manufacturing conditions. If manufacturing conditions, potential cross-contact between foods, and ingredient derivatives pose a risk for you, please reread all food labels and call the manufacturer to confirm potential allergen concerns BEFORE consumption. Ingredients and manufacturing practices can change overnight and without warning.

That being said, the following products are, to the best of my knowledge, allergy-free. Look for these products at your local natural foods store or grocery store, or order them online.

PRODUCT BRANDS

BEANS
Eden Organics
Canned, BPA-free
www.edenfoods.com

BEER
Bard's Tale Beer
www.bardbeer.com

Redbridge Beer
www.redbridgebeer.com

BREAD AND BUNS
(HAMBURGER AND HOT DOG BUNS)
Ener-G Foods
www.ener-g.com

Kinnikinnick
Not egg-free
www.kinnikinnick.com

Udi's Gluten-Free
Not egg-free
www.udisglutenfree.com

163

BREADCRUMBS (GLUTEN-FREE)
Ener-G
www.ener-g.com

Hol-Grain
www.holgrain.com

BROTH AND STOCK
Kitchen Basics
www.kitchenbasics.net

BROWN RICE FLOUR
Authentic Foods
Authentic Foods is my favorite brand of brown
rice flour, but for brown rice flour from a
dedicated allergy-free facility, see Ener-G, below.
www.glutenfree-supermarket.com

Ener-G foods
www.ener-g.com

BUTTERY SPREAD
Earth Balance
www.earthbalancenatural.com

CANOLA OIL
Crisco Canola Oil
www.crisco.com

CHEESE (VEGAN)
Daiya
Dairy-free, soy-free, vegan, and nut-free
www.daiyafoods.com

CHICKEN OR TURKEY
Trader Joe's
Canned, BPA-free
www.traderjoes.com

CHOCOLATE BARS
Enjoy Life Foods
Boom CHOCO Boom bars
www.enjoylifefoods.com

COCONUT AMINO ACIDS
Coconut Secret
www.coconutsecret.com

COCONUT MILK
Native Forest
BPA-free
www.edwardandsons.com

COCONUT MILK YOGURT
So Delicious Coconut Milk Yogurt
www.turtlemountain.com

CORN
Trader Joe's
Canned, BPA-free
www.traderjoes.com

CORNFLAKES
Erewhon Corn Flakes
www.attunefoods.com

CORNMEAL
Arrowhead Mills
www.arrowheadmills.com

CORNSTARCH
Let's Do...Organic
Organic, GMO-free
www.edwardandsons.com

EGG REPLACER
Ener-G Egg Replacer
www.ener-g.com

FLAXSEED MEAL
NOW Foods Organic Golden Flaxseed Meal
www.nowfoods.com

FLOUR BLEND
Authentic Foods GF Classical Blend
www.authenticfoods.com

GLUTEN-FREE BATTER
Choice Batter
www.choicebatter.com

HERBS AND SPICES
Spicely Organic Spices
www.spicely.com

HEMP SEEDS (HEMP HEARTS)
Manitoba Harvest
www.manitobaharvest.com

PASTA
Ancient Harvest
Corn/quinoa pasta
www.quinoa.net

Lundberg
Brown rice pasta
www.lundberg.com

Tinkyada
Brown rice pasta
www.tinkyada.com

Trader Joe's
Brown rice pasta, corn pasta
www.traderjoes.com

POTATO STARCH
Authentic Foods
Authentic Foods is my favorite brand of potato starch, but for potato starch from a dedicated allergy-free facility, see Ener-G, below.
www.glutenfree-supermarket.com

Ener-G Foods
www.ener-g.com

RICE MILK
Pacific Natural Foods
Pacific low-fat rice milk, plain
www.pacificfoods.com

Rice Dream
Enriched Original rice milk, plain (organic)
www.tastethedream.com

SUNFLOWER SEED BUTTER
SunButter
www.sunbutter.com

SUNFLOWER SEEDS
SunButter
Roasted and the only salted sunflower seeds that I know of that are processed in a dedicated nut-free facility.
www.peanutfreeplanet.com

TAPIOCA STARCH
Authentic Foods
Authentic Foods is my favorite brand of tapioca starch, but for tapioca starch from a dedicated allergy-free facility, see Ener-G, below.
www.glutenfree-supermarket.com

Ener-G Foods
www.ener-g.com

TOMATOES
Eden Organic
Tomatoes in glass jars
www.edenfoods.com

Muir Glen Organic
Canned, BPA-free
www.muirglen.com

Pomì Tomatoes
Tomatoes in aseptic cartons
www.pomi.us.com

Trader Joe's
Canned, BPA-free
www.traderjoes.com

TRUFFLE SALT
Williams-Sonoma
www.williams-sonoma.com

VEGAN SOY-FREE MAYONNAISE
Follow Your Heart
www.followyourheart.com

VEGETABLE SHORTENING
(DAIRY-FREE, SOY-FREE)
Spectrum Organic Shortening
www.spectrumorganics.com

XANTHAN GUM
Authentic Foods
Corn-free, dairy-free
www.glutenfree-supermarket.com

Ener-G Foods
Not corn-free
www.ener-g.com

ALLERGY-FREE / GLUTEN-FREE ONLINE STORES

AllerNeeds
www.bestallergysites.com

Divvies
www.divvies.com

Edward & Sons Trading Company
www.edwardandsons.com

Ener-G Foods
www.ener-g.com

Enjoy Life Foods
www.enjoylifefoods.com

FAB Snacks
www.fabsnacks.com

Glutenfree.com
www.glutenfree.com

The Gluten-Free Mall
www.glutenfreemall.com

MotherNature.com
www.mothernature.com

Nature's Flavors
www.naturesflavors.com

Navan Foods
www.navanfoods.com

No Nuttin' Foods Inc.
www.nonuttin.com

Peanut Free Planet
www.peanutfreeplanet.com

Solutions to Savor
www.solutionstosavor.com

Vermont Nut Free Chocolate Company
www.vermontnutfree.com

EQUIPMENT SOURCES

Amazon
www.amazon.com

Bed Bath & Beyond
www.bedbathandbeyond.com

Bridge Kitchenware
www.bridgekitchenware.com

Chef's Catalog Co.
www.chefscatalog.com

King Arthur Flour Tool Shop
www.kingarthurflour.com

Pastry Chef Central
www.pastrychef.com

Sur La Table
www.surlatable.com

Williams-Sonoma
www.williams-sonoma.com

ORGANIZATIONS PROVIDING SUPPORT *and* INFORMATION *for* PEOPLE *with* FOOD ALLERGIES *and* CELIAC DISEASE

AllerDine.com
www.allerdine.com

AllergicChild.com
www.allergicchild.com

Allergic Girl Resources, Inc.
www.allergicgirlresources.com

AllergyEats
www.allergyeats.com

AllergyFree Passport
www.allergyfreepassport.com

AllergyKids Foundation
www.allergykids.com

AllergyMoms
www.allergymoms.com

**American Academy of Allergy Asthma
& Immunology**
www.aaaai.org

American Academy of Pediatrics
www.aap.org

Anaphylaxis Canada
www.anaphylaxis.org

Asthma and Allergy Foundation of America
www.aafa.org

Attention Deficit Disorder Association
www.add.org

Autism Research Institute
www.autism.com

Autism Speaks
www.autismspeaks.org

Celiac Disease Foundation
www.celiac.org

Celiac Sprue Association
www.csaceliacs.org

Developmental Delay Resources
www.devdelay.org

Food Allergy & Anaphylaxis Network/
Food Allergy Initiative
www.foodallergy.org

Gluten Free Life
www.theglutenfreelife.com

GlutenFree Passport
www.glutenfreepassport.com

Gluten Intolerance Group
www.gluten.net

Go Dairy Free
www.godairyfree.org

International Foundation for
Functional Gastrointestinal Disorders
www.iffgd.org

Jaffe Food Allergy Institute,
Mount Sinai School of Medicine
www.mountsinai.org

Kids with Food Allergies Foundation
www.kidswithfoodallergies.org

My Food Facts
www.myfoodfacts.com

Onespot Allergy
www.onespotallergy.ca

University of Chicago Celiac Disease Center
www.celiacdisease.net

Index

Measurement Conversions

VOLUME

U.S.	IMPERIAL	METRIC
1 tablespoon	1/2 fl oz	15 ml
2 tablespoons	1 fl oz	30 ml
1/4 cup	2 fl oz	60 ml
1/3 cup	3 fl oz	90 ml
1/2 cup	4 fl oz	120 ml
2/3 cup	5 fl oz (1/4 pint)	150 ml
3/4 cup	6 fl oz	180 ml
1 cup	8 fl oz (1/3 pint)	240 ml
1 1/4 cups	10 fl oz (1/2 pint)	300 ml
2 cups (1 pint)	16 fl oz (2/3 pint)	480 ml
2 1/2 cups	20 fl oz (1 pint)	600 ml
1 quart	32 fl oz (1 2/3 pint)	1 l

TEMPERATURE

FAHRENHEIT	CELSIUS/GAS MARK
250°F	120°C/gas mark 1/2
275°F	135°C/gas mark 1
300°F	150°C/gas mark 2
325°F	160°C/gas mark 3
350°F	180 or 175°C/gas mark 4
375°F	190°C/gas mark 5
400°F	200°C/gas mark 6
425°F	220°C/gas mark 7
450°F	230°C/gas mark 8
475°F	245°C/gas mark 9
500°F	260°C

LENGTH

INCH	METRIC
1/4 inch	6 mm
1/2 inch	1.25 cm
3/4 inch	2 cm
1 inch	2.5 cm
6 inches (1/2 foot)	15 cm
12 inches (1 foot)	30 cm

WEIGHT

U.S./IMPERIAL	METRIC
1/2 oz	15 g
1 oz	30 g
2 oz	60 g
1/4 lb	115 g
1/3 lb	150 g
1/2 lb	225 g
3/4 lb	350 g
1 lb	450 g